THIS RESTLESS HOUSE

THE BOUGH BREAKS
ELECTRA AND HER SHADOW
Based on Aeschylus' *Oresteia*

by Zinnie Harris

‖SAMUEL FRENCH‖

FOR AMATEUR PRODUCTION ENQUIRIES

UNITED KINGDOM AND WORLD
EXCLUDING NORTH AMERICA
licensing@concordtheatricals.co.uk

020-7054-7200

Each title is subject to availability from Concord Theatricals, depending upon country of performance.

MUSIC USE NOTE

Licensees are solely responsible for obtaining formal written permission from copyright owners to use copyrighted music in the performance of this play and are strongly cautioned to do so. If no such permission is obtained by the licensee, then the licensee must use only original music that the licensee owns and controls. Licensees are solely responsible and liable for all music clearances and shall indemnify the copyright owners of the play(s) and their licensing agent, Concord Theatricals, against any costs, expenses, losses and liabilities arising from the use of music by licensees. Please contact the appropriate music licensing authority in your territory for the rights to any incidental music.

USE OF COPYRIGHT MUSIC

A licence issued by Concord Theatricals to perform this play does not include permission to use the incidental music specified in this copy. Where the place of performance is already licensed by the PERFORMING RIGHT SOCIETY (PRS) a return of the music used must be made to them. If the place of performance is not so licensed then application should be made to the PRS, 2 Pancras Square, London, N1C 4AG (www.prsformusic.com).A separate and additional licence from PHONOGRAPHIC PERFORMANCE LTD, 1 Upper James Street, London W1F 9DE (www.ppluk.com) is needed whenever commercial recordings are used.

IMPORTANT BILLING AND CREDIT REQUIREMENTS

If you have obtained performance rights to this title, please refer to your licensing agreement for important billing and credit requirements.

AUTHOR'S NOTE

The three plays that comprise *This Restless House* can be performed on their own or as part of a continuous evening. Together they run at 4.5 hours, and if performed in rep with each other, I suggest part one (*Agamemnon's Return*) plays on its own, then parts two and three (*The Bough Breaks* and *Electra And Her Shadow*) play as different parts of the same evening.

When we first performed this trilogy at the Citizens/National Theatre of Scotland we used ten actors in total plus four children. This meant that the chorus was made up of three actors. It would also work comfortably for larger casts, and then the chorus could be much more substantial. You can divide the chorus lines up however you wish, but they shouldn't speak as a whole group – rather as a bickering and discordant group of old and dishevelled men.

The style and staging is open to future directors; for the first production our references were the Balkan wars and the Eastern European revolutions of the late eighties; but whatever the setting, it should be messy and glamorous in a down-at-heel way and very bloody. There are various songs that should be sung by the chorus and /or the whole company. I have given lyrics, and these can be sung either to an original or existing tune – anything that feels folky and like it comes from the anarchic energy of the chorus.

All of the plays are about love in some way, and they work best if the love is there alongside all the darkness and hatred. Clytemnestra loves Agamemnon, and hence is so torn. Their scene on the hill, in the first play, is where they re-encounter that, and the question we had in rehearsal for that scene was whether or not these two people were ever going to be able to becomes lovers again. Equally in the second play, the starting point should be that Electra loves her mother, and the last thing she would ever do is to hurt her. Her journey is one of separation from her mother and seeing her as she is, rather than as she wants her to be. Also of course having to appease her father's ghost. (In Dominic Hill's production the ghost of Agamemnon was always visible, bloody and itchy in the background, sometimes coming and sitting among the action; this was very effective, but however you stage it, Agamemnon's influence should never feel far away.) In the third play, love is there too – finally – and at the last moments the little girl comes back on to stage with her suitcase; it should feel as if all the characters remember that love and gentleness have been the things they lost.

Zinnie Harris

THIS RESTLESS HOUSE

This Restless House first performed at the Citizens Theatre in May 2016.

CAST

AGAMEMNON	George Anton
DOCTOR/JORDAN	Adam Best
CHORUS/ IAN	Cliff Burnett
BUTCHER/CHORUS/MICHAEL	George Costigan
AEGISTHUS/CHORUS	Keith Fleming
CLYTEMNESTRA	Pauline Knowles
ORESTES	Lorn Macdonald
ELECTRA	Olivia Morgan
CELIA/MEGAN	Itxaso Moreno
AUDREY	Anita Vettesse
YOUNG ELECTRA	Chloe Chambers
YOUNG ELECTRA	Orla Hay
IPHIGENIA	Rose Hughes
IPHIGENIA	Freya Kane
OWEN	Jonas Lennie
OWEN	Callum McGhie

with Rich McPherson, Mike Moran, Loretta Scott, Annette Stewart and Stevie Thomson-Fitch

CREATIVE TEAM

Writer – Zinnie Harris
Director – Dominic Hill
Designer – Colin Richmond
Composer – Nikola Kodjabashia
Lighting Designer – Ben Ormerod
Movement Director – EJ Boyle
Fight Director – Emma Claire Brightlyn
Assistant Director – Jack Nurse

CHARACTERS

BUTCHER

A SERVING WOMAN CALLED CELIA

CLYTEMNESTRA

ELECTRA

AEGISTHUS

A DOCTOR

ORESTES

AGAMEMNON

AUDREY

JORDAN

MICHAEL

MEGAN

IAN

OWEN

IPHIGENIA

CHORUS

THE BOUGH BREAKS

Scene One

The palace BUTCHER *comes on to stage.*

He starts making a cup of tea.

BUTCHER the doctor said perhaps she was too hot
so we opened all the windows in the room
the doctor said perhaps she was too cold so we lit a fire
the doctor said try a little soup
so we made soup
try a little cold compress on the skin, he said
try a hot compress on the skin
try needles beneath the fingernails
feathers on the feet
trumpets in the ear
nothing
not one twitch
not a single moment where she sat up and looked at us
the doctor at least is honest, I have never seen this before
he said, it's a mystery
I read all the books, then I read them again

Beat.

so the king starts – this has to be sorted now
he puts a sign up in the town
has to be careful,
no one really likes them out there

there was celebrating I heard, the queen won't wake
thank fuck
let's light a fire dance around it
let's hope she dies that way
but the king puts on his notice
a huge reward
anyone that can rouse her from her sleep
they came then, they lined up outside the palace
little old women
little old men
the young, the weird
the slap-bang ordinary
try this, it woke my child
pray to this god, it cured the lame
try this
a different potion, a different prayer for every hour
none of it worked, of course
the king, by now in a temper
get out you stupid cretins
get out get out, can no one wake my wife?

Beat.

I should have introduced myself
I am the butcher here
I was the butcher, been the butcher since the age of ten
most of the staff ran that night
most of them couldn't get out of here fast enough
blood on the flagstones, get gone
but me
well, where else had I to go?

I was the butcher before

what was I going to be after?

I am the cook, the cleaner now

anything needs doing

I make her a cup of tea every hour

on the hour so that when she wakes

well she'll be thirsty after a sleep like that.

A serving woman, CELIA, *comes in.*

She looks at the BUTCHER, *he looks at her.*

CELIA don't know why you bother

BUTCHER don't start

CELIA Seventeen days, the situation is clear

BUTCHER she'll wake up

CELIA tff.

you said that yesterday and the day before

if she was going to wake she would have done by now

CELIA *picks up a pile of sheets and goes out.*

you should be digging a grave not making the tea.

The BUTCHER *is left with the cup and saucer.*

Scene Two

In the Queen's bedroom.

The BUTCHER *brings in the cup of tea.*

ELECTRA is watching her mother.

The BUTCHER *puts down the tea.*

He starts to go.

ELECTRA please don't just leave

The BUTCHER *looks uncomfortable.*

BUTCHER where's the king?

ELECTRA the king is no use

you are the closest she's got to a friend

He looks at her.

I mean, I know I'm not supposed to talk to staff but

I've been here for ten hours

on my own

and

my mother is fond of you

I know you work in the kitchen

BUTCHER worked there all my life

ELECTRA I know that night five years ago

you cleaned the flagstones

Beat.

I know everyone else ran pretty much but you got out a
bucket and cleaned the blood off the flagstones

you didn't need to

Beat.

and I know you put me to bed

I don't remember anything of that night, but my mum told me

she pointed you out in the garden one day when you were dragging a calf and said that man there, he put you to bed that night

that dreadful night

he is one you can trust

he lifted you up from the flagstones once he had finished cleaning them and he carried you up to your room

Beat.

BUTCHER I only did

ELECTRA I just mean –

that was nice

I might have stayed out there all night if it wasn't for you

Beat.

you're different to the rest

oh they do what they are told but they

well you get the feeling they despise us

but you

for some reason you aren't like that

Beat.

she looks exactly the same doesn't she? No better no worse

BUTCHER stay hopeful

ELECTRA even the doctor –

BUTCHER everyone wakes up in the end

they'll sort it

ELECTRA it would be better if we were a normal family
    things like this happen in a normal family and you can go,
    ok
    this is something to do with the body
    the blood or the veins something in the sinews
    this belongs in the physical world
    but in our family

BUTCHER the doctor will find a cure

ELECTRA the king is thinking of sacking the doctor
    he has no patience
    he will be imprisoned and beaten before long

BUTCHER he'll get another doctor, a better doctor

ELECTRA we both know what this is.
    don't look at me like that I'm not an idiot
    this is a haunting.

    Beat.

BUTCHER Electra –

ELECTRA don't tell me it isn't
    you of all people should know that
    it started on the anniversary, three years to the day
    I can't be the only one that noticed that

BUTCHER I think you should talk to the king

ELECTRA the king is stupid, can only see what the king sees
    I say to him this is a haunting, he'll laugh in my face
    you know where the grave is

BUTCHER Electra

ELECTRA I love my mother, I won't let her die
    and the stupid doctor can't offer her anything

she needs us to end this

BUTCHER how?

ELECTRA by going to the grave

by calling the ghost

Beat.

BUTCHER you know talk of ghosts is out-lawed

ELECTRA I know

BUTCHER the gods don't like it.

once a spirit has crossed the river that is that. Men do not

come back to earth to do ill

ELECTRA and yet you hear of it

BUTCHER those are stories, older stories.

the two are incompatible

your father is in the underworld

he cannot harm anyone

ELECTRA and yet he does.

Beat.

BUTCHER your mother in particular is very clear about the gods

she is a devout observer now. Look at the shrines to Athena

she has here in her room

ELECTRA she wasn't always, she used to laugh at the gods

she told me about a ghost who sat on her shoulder once

Beat.

BUTCHER we couldn't even get to the grave

no one is allowed out of the palace grounds

you know you step out you might get killed

ELECTRA another objection

BUTCHER that the king has given these orders

ELECTRA the king again

BUTCHER there are enemies all around

people plotting –

ELECTRA we can be safe, we'll cover our heads

we'll go in disguise

if she would just bloody wake on her own ok, but

I have to go to the grave

listen you either believe it or not

you either see things in one way or another

I'm not asking you to believe it, I'm just asking you to take

me to the grave

BUTCHER if I get caught, I am a servant here

ELECTRA I am no better

BUTCHER the king won't punish you

ELECTRA you think?

you don't know how cruel the king can be

it's an unmarked grave, I won't find it without you

He hesitates.

forget it then.

please excuse me, I thought you were someone you're not.

I have finished my tea.

She hands him back her cup.

BUTCHER I didn't say that

ELECTRA so what did you say?

AEGISTHUS *comes in.*

AEGISTHUS time for you to go

ELECTRA aren't you going to ask how she is?

He takes his shoes off and gets on to the bed.

AEGISTHUS a little worse by the looks of things

ELECTRA she is exactly the same

He looks at **CLYTEMNESTRA.**

AEGISTHUS a little worse

did you move my stuff off the bed?

ELECTRA no

AEGISTHUS my nightshirt, I sleep here

why is my stuff on the floor?

ELECTRA it fell

AEGISTHUS what, she rolled over and it fell?

ELECTRA I moved it a little, I thought she looked uncomfortable

AEGISTHUS don't touch her

I told you before, she isn't yours

AEGISTHUS *cuddles into her.*

she seems worse

what did you do to her?

ELECTRA nothing, I spoke to her that's all

AEGISTHUS you spoke to her?

ELECTRA yes. I spoke to her all day

AEGISTHUS what did you say then?

if it was words that did this, then they must have been
poisonous

ELECTRA she is no different

AEGISTHUS I don't think you should be alone with her any more

ELECTRA what?

AEGISTHUS I think only the doctors and I should attend to
her from now on

ELECTRA she is my mother

AEGISTHUS and she is my wife

I am in charge in this house

ELECTRA she is in charge

AEGISTHUS she is asleep

I think it's better if you stay away

you're making her worse by your presence, I don't know
how but

ELECTRA she is exactly the same as this morning

AEGISTHUS are you arguing with me?

ELECTRA no

AEGISTHUS I'll decide what is best for her

thank you

stay away Electra or I will keep you out.

ELECTRA you can't do that

AEGISTHUS I am king here

you were tolerated while your mother was here, but now
she's not.

ELECTRA she is here

AEGISTHUS she is asleep.

Beat.

and while she sleeps

ELECTRA I hate you.

AEGISTHUS I think I'll live

now get out of here before I call someone to remove you.

ELECTRA no

AEGISTHUS no?

ELECTRA she is my mother, I'll stay here

AEGISTHUS oh so you want me to use some force?

> **AEGISTHUS** *slaps* **ELECTRA**. **ELECTRA**'s *face stings.*

> **ELECTRA** *picks up the tea cup to throw, the* **BUTCHER**
> *intervenes to stop her.*

BUTCHER come Electra come with me

ELECTRA I hate him

BUTCHER don't fight

we've got things to do.

come on.

AEGISTHUS a wise servant with some sense

shut the door behind you

BUTCHER come on

> *The* **BUTCHER** *takes* **ELECTRA**'s *hand.*

Scene Three

The BUTCHER *and* ELECTRA *are outside.*

BUTCHER families can be difficult places

a new father on the scene

ELECTRA he isn't my father, and he isn't that new

BUTCHER your mother ill

just let me catch my breath

He looks about.

ELECTRA I wish someone would kill him

you say we have enemies

I would open the door

BUTCHER they hate your mother worse, sorry to say

ELECTRA I know

BUTCHER he'll settle down

when your mother is better. You know the truth?

he is as worried as you, he doesn't know how to handle it

ELECTRA and me, why should I be the one who knows how to handle it?

BUTCHER keep your voice down

if anyone heard us talking like this –

ELECTRA there's no one around

BUTCHER oh they'll be out there

watching

and when they ask

ELECTRA you're paranoid

BUTCHER you are my grand-daughter

when anyone asks

we've come out for a walk

ELECTRA *doesn't answer.*

we aren't looking for anything in particular

we like nature

butterflies in fact

we like walking through the fields

ELECTRA this is crazy –

BUTCHER looking for butterflies

that's why we are here

we are out enjoying a day in the fields

ELECTRA what would they do? These people

BUTCHER me? They would string me up from the nearest tree

for my loyalty to the queen

you?

I don't like to think what they would do to you.

ELECTRA why have we stopped?

BUTCHER I'm trying to remember

it is one of these

ELECTRA here?

BUTCHER of these three

two

it could be this one or that one

ELECTRA you don't remember?

BUTCHER it was dark

we didn't have long, we had to move him, we knew there'd

be trouble

The **BUTCHER** *looks around.*

we marked it with a few stones but I

He looks at the ground.

ELECTRA it isn't going to work if we aren't even sure

BUTCHER I can't guarantee

ELECTRA so what, am I supposed to pour wine into all the
mounds on this stretch?

BUTCHER you asked me to take you to the grave

ELECTRA yes to the grave
not to the general vicinity

BUTCHER I wish you would keep your voice down

ELECTRA there is no one
I can't see a single person, look
it's in your mind

BUTCHER they'll be hiding, they won't be in full view
they'll be watching us though

ELECTRA *looks around.*

ELECTRA well I don't care
hello world
string us up if you want, I am not going to hide

BUTCHER stop it, this isn't a joke
why are you so fearless?

ELECTRA is that a crime?

BUTCHER sit down.
please, now we are here, let's do it quickly.

ELECTRA *sits down and undoes her bag.*

ELECTRA I haven't exactly thought through what I am going
to say so

you are going to have to give me a little leeway

BUTCHER of course

ELECTRA I wasn't talking to you

She takes out some wine and some oil.

thing is

She pauses for a second to consider what to say.

ok we hardly know each other

and the things I know aren't good

but, you are my dad and

this has to stop

whatever it is you are doing, could you stop?

ELECTRA *is suddenly self-conscious.*

maybe I should sing, do you think I should sing?

BUTCHER bit noisy –

ELECTRA how can I talk to him? I don't know him

BUTCHER say the first thing that comes into your head

ELECTRA it would be easiest of all if I could say she was sorry

she didn't mean it

she lost her head and went crazy

BUTCHER so say she is sorry

ELECTRA but, she isn't

is she?

she thinks the gods have damned her but

she has told everyone she would do it again

and he believes –

BUTCHER he's dead

ELECTRA I know

Beat.

ELECTRA *looks at the grave.*

what was he like?

BUTCHER complicated

ELECTRA no difference there then.

maybe this was dumb

he doesn't know me, I don't know him

maybe there isn't much I can say actually

BUTCHER you can soothe

ELECTRA with what?

BUTCHER with being here

we came this far

Beat.

The **BUTCHER** *sits down beside her.*

you're doing well

Beat.

ELECTRA Dad

I...

Dad I guess

I don't understand you and I don't understand her

but could you be calmer ?

let go a bit

do something about your anger

there must be better things to do over there

fun things

new things

can't you go and do some of those?

you were loved, I think

you are loved even

there is nothing to be gained by taking her too

I need her here

I need her to be well

here

because if I don't have her –

so leave her now, please

and let her wake up

that's what I came to say. Dad.

really, that is all

I lost my sister, I lost you

I don't want to lose my mum as well.

Beat.

do you think that's ok?

BUTCHER I think that's probably ok

ELECTRA do I have to pour the rest of the wine in?

BUTCHER you might as well

ELECTRA maybe we should have brought more

I don't like the way it makes the ground sort of bubble

BUTCHER what was that?

ELECTRA what?

The **BUTCHER** *stands up.*

BUTCHER I heard a noise

ELECTRA just me

clinking the bottle

BUTCHER if someone is coming

ELECTRA where? There's nothing

BUTCHER over there

　get down Electra hide behind the mound

ELECTRA there's no one

BUTCHER we don't know who is watching

　seriously there are enemies

　someone is watching us and making a noise

　you might be fearless but I don't actually want to die

　particularly in the barbaric way of our enemies' choosing

ELECTRA this is my father's grave I am not afraid

　it's the bell you can hear

BUTCHER what bell?

ELECTRA the bell from the palace

He stands up.

BUTCHER what?

They listen.

ELECTRA something has happened.

Scene Four

CLYTEMNESTRA *is standing up.*

The serving woman, CELIA, *is changing her from her nightdress.*

AEGISTHUS *and the* DOCTOR *are in attendance.*

CLYTEMNESTRA I feel –

She tries again.

I feel –

AEGISTHUS maybe don't try and speak just yet

DOCTOR take your time

CLYTEMNESTRA I'm a little thirsty, could I have a glass of water?

AEGISTHUS bring some water

CLYTEMNESTRA and maybe some fruit

A glass of water is brought.

I feel –

DOCTOR drink the water first

She drinks the water.

CLYTEMNESTRA I feel absolutely –

AEGISTHUS and not dizzy?

CLYTEMNESTRA not dizzy no

AEGISTHUS your pulse

please take her pulse

The DOCTOR *feels for her pulse.*

DOCTOR normal

AEGISTHUS she has a normal pulse?

DOCTOR it's remarkable

CLYTEMNESTRA my fingernails have grown I feel like I want
a bath

AEGISTHUS can he see your teeth?
look at her teeth, look in her mouth
look at her all over

CLYTEMNESTRA is this necessary?

AEGISTHUS he must check all possibilities

She shows her teeth.

DOCTOR her mouth looks normal

AEGISTHUS show him your hands

CLYTEMNESTRA I feel like an animal
are you sure I slept as long as you said?

DOCTOR she has a slight sweat on her palms

AEGISTHUS is that a catastrophe?

CLYTEMNESTRA is that all?

DOCTOR I can't find a single thing wrong with you
you seem

CLYTEMNESTRA I do have a slight headache

AEGISTHUS she has a headache
did you hear that?

CLYTEMNESTRA it's minor

The DOCTOR looks at her.

DOCTOR it's remarkable
a slight headache

AEGISTHUS will you note that?

DOCTOR it's noted

CLYTEMNESTRA can I get dressed now, can I walk about?

Beat.

AEGISTHUS do you think it is wise?

after so many days, to get up

DOCTOR do you feel you want to?

AEGISTHUS does it matter if she wants to?

CLYTEMNESTRA I've been lying down so long I think it would be good

DOCTOR then yes, I can't see any reason

AEGISTHUS are you sure?

I mean, she is precious I don't want to

DOCTOR sir, I believe your wife is fine.

AEGISTHUS *takes this in.*

AEGISTHUS really?

DOCTOR yes.

He smiles.

AEGISTHUS you're fine?

CLYTEMNESTRA apparently I am.

He smiles and they sort of laugh together.

AEGISTHUS *comes and kisses her.*

AEGISTHUS you sir will be well rewarded, whatever you want just don't go too far, stay close if you would

DOCTOR of course

The **DOCTOR** *starts to retreat.*

AEGISTHUS *kisses her again.*

AEGISTHUS I missed you

you don't know how worried I was

I am so relieved I can't tell you

CLYTEMNESTRA there's a fly on my shirt

DOCTOR I'll leave you now, if you need me

AEGISTHUS thank you doctor

CLYTEMNESTRA can you get it off?

AEGISTHUS just a fly

CLYTEMNESTRA you know I hate flies

He brushes it off.

AEGISTHUS well done for waking up my love

I missed you,

I need you

ELECTRA *rushes in.*

ELECTRA Mum

CLYTEMNESTRA my baby

ELECTRA *runs to hug her.*

darling

ELECTRA I thought you'd die

AEGISTHUS don't crowd her

CLYTEMNESTRA she's ok

AEGISTHUS your mother has been extremely ill

I don't think you should rush at her like that

CLYTEMNESTRA it's fine

AEGISTHUS the doctor said –

ELECTRA are you really ok?

CLYTEMNESTRA I am, I think, completely normal.

apart from a slight headache

ELECTRA *laughs.*

ELECTRA will you come outside with me?

CLYTEMNESTRA now?

ELECTRA why not?

CLYTEMNESTRA *looks at* **AEGISTHUS.**

CLYTEMNESTRA shall we all go outside?

AEGISTHUS I think it's a bit wet to go outside

you've been extremely unwell

ELECTRA the rain has passed

AEGISTHUS but underfoot

ELECTRA she can wear some shoes

CLYTEMNESTRA I could just go out for a minute, couldn't I?

AEGISTHUS and then?

risk ill health

Beat.

CLYTEMNESTRA I'll come out later Electra love

Beat.

ELECTRA then I'll stay indoors

AEGISTHUS no reason why you shouldn't go outside

ELECTRA I'll stay with her

CLYTEMNESTRA good, all three of us together.

She takes both of their hands.

I love you both

AEGISTHUS I have some work to do.

CLYTEMNESTRA now?

AEGISTHUS yes now.

I'll see you later.

AEGISTHUS *leaves them.*

CLYTEMNESTRA *watches him go. Worried.*

She hugs **ELECTRA.**

Scene Five

The BUTCHER *is in the kitchen making a cup of tea.*

CELIA what are you doing?

BUTCHER I make this every hour

CELIA she's woken up now

BUTCHER I know but

CELIA *takes the cup out of his hand.*

CELIA it's over

BUTCHER maybe she would still like a cup of tea

CELIA she's in the garden with her daughter
look

The BUTCHER *looks.*

do you ever think you care too much, that you are too
involved?

BUTCHER I've been here a long time that's all

CELIA it's more than that
it's like you think of them before you think of yourself
everyone else ran but you

BUTCHER I had nowhere else to go

CELIA you had plenty of places
I know your sister
she'd have taken you in like a shot
you couldn't go
something about you

BUTCHER and?
you say that like it is a character flaw

CELIA it's an observation.

you're different to me

and no good comes of it, that's all.

you get too close to a family like this you get shat on.

always.

come on I'll make you a cup of tea.

Scene Six

AEGISTHUS *and* CLYTEMNESTRA *are at dinner.*

Some formality to the dining room, but otherwise the atmosphere is drab.

AEGISTHUS how are you now?

CLYTEMNESTRA you need to stop fussing

AEGISTHUS just tell me you are still fine

CLYTEMNESTRA I am still fine

AEGISTHUS remarkable.

Beat.

CLYTEMNESTRA where's Electra?

I thought Electra might be joining us

AEGISTHUS no, did you want her?

I just thought

well, some time alone, just the –

CLYTEMNESTRA oh

Beat.

AEGISTHUS do you mind?

CLYTEMNESTRA not at all.

that's lovely.

Beat.

where will she eat?

AEGISTHUS she'll eat in the kitchen

she seems to like the staff and

well it's late for Electra, you always say she goes to bed too

late so I thought tonight

CLYTEMNESTRA you are so thoughtful

> *Beat.*

AEGISTHUS shall I serve?

CLYTEMNESTRA thank you.

AEGISTHUS how much would you like?

CLYTEMNESTRA some

> *He serves her.*
>
> *He serves himself.*
>
> *He tucks in.*
>
> *She doesn't.*
>
> *He looks at her.*
>
> *She looks at him.*
>
> *They smile.*
>
> *Then he starts eating again.*
>
> *She doesn't.*

AEGISTHUS something wrong?

CLYTEMNESTRA no

> *She tries again.*

AEGISTHUS is it too greasy?

too cold, do you want me to get them to heat it up?

CLYTEMNESTRA no I...

> *Beat.*

there's an insect of some sort in fact

AEGISTHUS where?

CLYTEMNESTRA here

> on my plate

AEGISTHUS I'll get that imbecile in the kitchen beaten

CLYTEMNESTRA no

AEGISTHUS he won't sit down for a week

CLYTEMNESTRA don't do that.

> *She holds the insect up on her fork.*

> it's interesting that is all
> another fly

> **AEGISTHUS** *reaches over and takes the fly off her plate.*

AEGISTHUS there it's gone

> *She looks down at her plate.*

> *She starts to eat.*

> you know while you were away

CLYTEMNESTRA I wasn't away

AEGISTHUS I mean asleep

> it was like you were away
> while you were asleep
> I tried to keep things going but
> I actually had no appetite
> the things about governance came up, several things
> I realized I

CLYTEMNESTRA and now there is another

AEGISTHUS what?

CLYTEMNESTRA there's another fly

AEGISTHUS the same one

CLYTEMNESTRA no another, here
in my food

He stops, he looks over at her plate.

AEGISTHUS I can't see it

CLYTEMNESTRA you can't see that?

He looks.

AEGISTHUS it's tiny

CLYTEMNESTRA I had this dream

AEGISTHUS can I talk to you about the governance?

CLYTEMNESTRA sorry

AEGISTHUS no go on, your dream

CLYTEMNESTRA I dreamt I was being chased by flies
all over the fields
I was outside the palace
walking through the fields
hot day
but these flies
and the more I ran the more there were of them

AEGISTHUS just a dream

CLYTEMNESTRA I know but

Beat.

then the first thing I saw when I opened my eyes that fly
on my shirt

AEGISTHUS it's May

CLYTEMNESTRA three flies in a short space of time

AEGISTHUS you should see the flies around the cattle at this
time of year

CLYTEMNESTRA I know

AEGISTHUS we all have dreams

whatever that sleep was, well it was odd

CLYTEMNESTRA there's something rotten here

why was it my plate that they fell on and not yours

why was it my sleeve?

AEGISTHUS I think you are reading too much into this

CLYTEMNESTRA I am damned, I know I am damned

the gods have told me I am damned but

now

well why are the flies attracted to me not you?

AEGISTHUS you're confused, maybe you are still coming out
of your sleep

CLYTEMNESTRA I never felt more awake

apart from this damn headache

She stands up.

look there they are on the ceiling

they are waiting for me ready to pounce

what brings flies but dead flesh?

that was what the dream was telling me

I'm going to be dead soon

AEGISTHUS listen we can call a seer

CLYTEMNESTRA I don't need a seer

AEGISTHUS there might be an alternative explanation

CLYTEMNESTRA to what?

the gods have condemned me for my crime

She puts a hand out.

see they fly towards me now

AEGISTHUS you know this talk is really turning my stomach

ok so you were tired or had some illness but now

there is nothing wrong with you madam the doctor said himself

CLYTEMNESTRA so why are they all around me?

AEGISTHUS they aren't

there is nothing around you but imagination.

CLYTEMNESTRA the gods

AEGISTHUS the gods nothing, it was necessary what you did

sit back down

She doesn't.

alright, let us eat standing up.

He stands up.

He holds his plate.

I try with you

I really do

you've been asleep for over two weeks, don't you think that might have been a little hard for me too?

don't you think I might have been a bit worried about you?

don't you think I might have been dumped with the governance and your daughter and you sleeping sweetly?

I'm not saying I mind it is just

now you're awake

now you are awake

Beat.

I thought this could be a little time for us

CLYTEMNESTRA even if the gods have made me rot?

AEGISTHUS you aren't rotting. That's the point

you know I wish you would just say what is actually going
on here.

you don't want to spend time with me

you might as well be honest

this is nothing to do with the gods

even an evening, even the short distance of a meal is too
much for you to bear

CLYTEMNESTRA that isn't true

AEGISTHUS you asked about Electra, you would prefer her to
be here

CLYTEMNESTRA she is my daughter

AEGISTHUS even before you went to sleep things were difficult
we both know it

at the start it was bearable perhaps with some moments of
lightness but after that, these past three years

CLYTEMNESTRA yes we had problems but

AEGISTHUS it was more than that.

Beat.

you won't even look at me now

this evening since you woke up

CLYTEMNESTRA I'll look at you

AEGISTHUS when asked

I tried to kiss you before you turned your head

CLYTEMNESTRA Electra was there

AEGISTHUS Electra is always there

I am not blind, when I touch you you shiver, when I come
near you you back away

CLYTEMNESTRA you're too sensitive

AEGISTHUS tell me I am wrong then

CLYTEMNESTRA can we not just eat our meal?

AEGISTHUS if we could just eat yes

>   my point exactly

>   if we could eat then yes

CLYTEMNESTRA do you mind if I take my leave?

>   I have a headache and this conversation –

AEGISTHUS I mind very much.

>   *Beat.*

CLYTEMNESTRA then fuck you

AEGISTHUS and what do the gods make of language like that?

>   *Beat.*

CLYTEMNESTRA alright you tell me what other meaning can there be in these flies?

AEGISTHUS for fuck's sake, enough!

CLYTEMNESTRA why are you so angry?

AEGISTHUS you know what I really think? All this I am troubled, I don't sleep, I sleep too long, I have dreams, the flies, the gods, I must atone

>   you never believed any of that shit

CLYTEMNESTRA but I was wrong

AEGISTHUS bollocks – it's an act

>   you want me to believe you are crazed, bewildered

>   you see meaning where there is none

>   I won't fall for it

CLYTEMNESTRA what do you mean?

AEGISTHUS you want to keep me out

CLYTEMNESTRA it is always about sex

AEGISTHUS yes I desire you

I am your husband I want you

badly, I want you

CLYTEMNESTRA and me? If I am not in the mood

AEGISTHUS you are never in the mood, that is just it.

CLYTEMNESTRA that isn't true

AEGISTHUS then prove me wrong.

CLYTEMNESTRA you will excuse me. I have tired of this conversation.

AEGISTHUS of course you have

CLYTEMNESTRA *walks out.*

I fucking love you, you know that.

I just want you to love me back

He smashes the flowers over.

Scene Seven

Later. In the middle of the night.

CLYTEMNESTRA *goes downstairs to the kitchen.*

CLYTEMNESTRA hello?

She looks around.

is anyone awake?

The woman comes.

I'm looking for the butcher

CELIA he...

CLYTEMNESTRA I realize it is late

it's the middle of the night

and I understand he might be asleep

but could you wake him

The woman stops for a second.

please

The woman goes.

CLYTEMNESTRA *looks around the kitchen.*

She looks at the knives.

She doesn't like the look of them.

She moves the block further away from herself.

*The **BUTCHER** comes out, dishevelled, pulling a cardigan over his night gear.*

BUTCHER madam

I am sorry I am –

CLYTEMNESTRA I can't sleep

BUTCHER that isn't surprising

CLYTEMNESTRA I know, of course I have slept too much but
in the past you have made me a little poultice

BUTCHER a poultice?

CLYTEMNESTRA I don't mind not sleeping but
something to relax perhaps
when I needed to...
some herbs or something
in the old days I would drink but obviously

BUTCHER of course

CLYTEMNESTRA or maybe I could just sit with you
the house is asleep

BUTCHER it's the middle of the night

CLYTEMNESTRA I know
some herbs then
a poultice yes please

BUTCHER I'll start right now

He looks around.

He gets a knife out.

She watches him.

CLYTEMNESTRA I can smell this awful stench

BUTCHER in here?

CLYTEMNESTRA everywhere
and it comes from me

BUTCHER no

CLYTEMNESTRA it's like my flesh is starting to rot, I told the king but he

She holds out her arm.

can you smell it?

BUTCHER you want me to smell?

CLYTEMNESTRA yes of course, smell

The BUTCHER *smells.*

BUTCHER nothing

CLYTEMNESTRA smell again

BUTCHER I am smelling

CLYTEMNESTRA the flies can smell it. It doesn't matter if you can or not

BUTCHER what flies?

CLYTEMNESTRA I always knew I would have to die

we always know that

it's the human condition to know that one day all this will be gone but

I thought I would have a little more time

I thought I would be able to raise Electra

BUTCHER you will

CLYTEMNESTRA I thought I would be able to pray hard and make amends

BUTCHER of course

CLYTEMNESTRA I thought I would go to my grave not as damned as I am

I thought I would be forgiven

but my death now

well, eternity is a long time to be dragging my soul

what will they do to me if I am to die now?

BUTCHER who?

CLYTEMNESTRA the gods.

that's who has sent the smell

they're telling me my time is up

BUTCHER madam I think this is just interpretation

CLYTEMNESTRA I know as clearly as I know anything.

will you look after Electra?

He puts the knife back down.

BUTCHER of course I will.

CLYTEMNESTRA you dropped something

BUTCHER where?

CLYTEMNESTRA there you dropped it

pick it up

if the gods are saying my time is coming

you can't be dropping things

BUTCHER I didn't drop anything

CLYTEMNESTRA sorry I thought you did

it's me then

it's me that is dropping things

She stoops down. She sees that there is nothing there.

She stands back up.

I don't want to die yet.

Scene Eight

Next morning.

ELECTRA *goes back to the grave. She is alone this time.*

ELECTRA that wasn't supposed to happen.
if that was some sort of joke
I didn't ask you to wake her just to make her worse
what the hell are you doing?
I brought more wine, I don't know if that was what you
wanted
or the men in the garden said you preferred spirits
so
here, get drunk
spend eternity in a stupor
please don't do this
I'm calling on you ghost
this is not fair, if this is a joke

A MAN *calls over from a little way away.*

MAN you shouldn't be here

ELECTRA I...

MAN no one should be here
do you know how dangerous it is?

ELECTRA I was just –

MAN what?

ELECTRA resting

MAN here?

ELECTRA I've walked miles today

MAN and you chose this spot?

ELECTRA it's a patch of ground isn't it?

MAN then you are almost as stupid as you look

    run girl

    this isn't a place to rest

    these graves are

    the men buried here

ELECTRA thieves and murderers I know

MAN this is the most damned place in the whole land

ELECTRA I know that too

MAN and still you stay

    The MAN picks up the wine.

    bit young for wine aren't you?

ELECTRA I'm older than I look

    He hands it back.

MAN appeasing ghosts with wine, an out-lawed art

ELECTRA it's a picnic

MAN oh I see, a picnic

    a girl like you, and a liquid picnic

    someone finds you here, they'll string you up.

    why are you bringing a peace offering to this grave?

ELECTRA the same reason you are standing here.

    Beat.

MAN I am standing here telling you to go away

    I am standing here, saving your life

ELECTRA fine

MAN you were here yesterday
    with an old man

ELECTRA a friend of mine

MAN I saw you both, this isn't a picnic and this isn't you resting

ELECTRA which is hers?
    I heard he was buried with a slave woman
    also murdered

MAN you seem to know a lot about this

ELECTRA my mother told me

MAN and who is your mother?

ELECTRA just a woman from the village

    Beat.

    their story is kind of famous

    ELECTRA *puts flowers on the grave.*

    She pours a little of the wine.

    can I sit for a second?

MAN you seem to have already

    She sits on something.

ELECTRA oh

    She finds what she is sitting on.

    It's a wax image.

MAN don't touch that
    they are laid out in a pattern

ELECTRA who is it of?

MAN the queen
    it brings bad luck to the queen

I believe

ELECTRA *looks at it.*

ELECTRA who would do such a thing?

MAN plenty

Beat.

ELECTRA poor queen then

MAN the most hated woman in the land
her husband was loved and then she killed him so
of course she is hated

ELECTRA and no one has sympathy for her

MAN not many, she's a murderess
do you?

ELECTRA of course not

Beat.

and you?

MAN certainly not

Beat.

ELECTRA it doesn't look like her anyway

MAN you've seen her then?

ELECTRA hasn't everyone?

MAN not for a while
they say that she drinks herself stupid

ELECTRA not any more

MAN you seem to know an awful lot about her.

Beat.

ELECTRA people have got her wrong

    she lost a girl

MAN I know about that

ELECTRA she killed the king because of the girl

MAN you've been sent from the palace, haven't you?

    you have palace written all over you, who are you a serving

    girl?

ELECTRA no

MAN a spy then, to see what the enemies are saying

ELECTRA definitely not

MAN just like the queen to send a girl

    get away from here or they'll kill you

    that man you were with, I recognized him

    he's the butcher

    he's from the palace too

ELECTRA how did you recognize him if you have never been

    there?

MAN don't try to trick me

ELECTRA I know you who you are

MAN unlikely

She pulls her cloak down.

ELECTRA we have the same hair

    the same complexion

MAN it's common around here

ELECTRA we have the same eyes

    the same hands

MAN who the fuck do you think you are?

ELECTRA I am Electra who are you?

MAN Electra is just a baby

ELECTRA I was

then I grew up

Beat.

MAN Electra?

ELECTRA Orestes?

Beat.

I've been waiting to see you

all these months through all this

no one talks about you

I say what about my brother, they say

ORESTES Orestes has gone

no one can find him

ELECTRA yes that's what they say

ORESTES you should believe them

ELECTRA I don't though

ORESTES finish what you need to do then go.

it's better that we don't talk

ELECTRA why?

Beat.

ORESTES we do have the same hair

the same complexion

ELECTRA it's like a mirror

ORESTES go away Electra forget that you have seen me

ELECTRA Mum isn't well

the ghost is –

ORESTES don't talk to me about the ghost

the ghost?

you think I don't know about the ghost

ELECTRA you too?

ORESTES I heard these stories

there are so many that wish her ill, I could hardly stop

hearing these tales

I would be in a town having a drink and someone would say

it falls to you now

the father is dead he can't avenge himself

ha ha I would go, back to my drink

then someone else, it's up to you

and someone else – just say the word

shut up I would say

I am not a hero

I love my mother

I had to move, keep moving

wherever I went people would say they would build an

army for me

they were right behind me I just had to say the word

I love my mother I said

I love my mother

I moved again

I moved land, I crossed the sea

I found a place, far from anywhere

they didn't know me

then it started

just an itch at first

here on my feet

everyone gets itches I thought

I scratched a bit, thought nothing of it

then the other foot

good grief that's itchy

it keep me awake a bit

it keeps me awake a lot, I hardly sleep now because of the

itches

ELECTRA maybe you need some cream

ORESTES you think I haven't tried cream?

I haven't tried every cream?

then the behind the ears, it started as well

on my back

you have no idea how it itches

I tore my clothes off

ELECTRA I don't understand

ORESTES you never knew him

of course I forget that

for you he was always away at war

but for me, when I was little he was there

he was always itchy

he had these scabs on his feet

it used to drive him crazy

you ask anyone

what was it that kept him awake during the nights at Troy,

fear of death, the pain of battle wounds?

no it was the itchy feet, and the back

if it was just the itches well ok but

he had a scar on his side where they took his appendix out

I have still got my appendix

my appendix has not been taken out but look

He lifts up his top.

He has a scar.

ELECTRA you sound like my mother

ORESTES he had two tattoos one on each arm
on one arm it said the name of the city on the other the
name of his wife

ORESTES *pulls up his sleeves.*

There are markings coming through.

ELECTRA what?

ORESTES you can almost read the words
I am turning into him
there is no other explanation
I have never had a tattoo
and I get these rages

ELECTRA dear Orestes

ORESTES no, it is not something that can be soothed by wine or
libation
the ghost also knows it falls to me
it falls to me Electra
the ghost cannot avenge itself
so it falls to me

ELECTRA I have itchy feet too
I think you are making too much of this
so, we are his children, he has an affliction then it follows
that we would

ORESTES I have never had my appendix out

ELECTRA *lifts up her top.*

She also has a scar.

She looks at **ORESTES.**

ELECTRA I have never actually noticed
maybe I always had that

ORESTES it isn't just me
it is both of us!
you have it too

ELECTRA I love my mother

ORESTES so do I.

ELECTRA *looks at her scar.*

ELECTRA I don't believe in ghosts

ORESTES then what the fuck are you doing here?

ELECTRA *is frightened now.*

I told you it was best that you hadn't seen me

ELECTRA I won't hurt her

ORESTES of course not, but the ghost won't stop until we do.

Scene Nine

ELECTRA *is alone. Back at the palace.*

She takes off her clothes.

She looks at herself in the mirror.

She has a scar.

She has a rash on her arms.

She is itchy all over.

She looks at her hands.

CLYTEMNESTRA *comes in.*

CLYTEMNESTRA there is a thing
I told them we shouldn't open the windows
the windows are no longer to be opened in the palace
because of the wildlife. Outside.
Electra
don't open the windows and

CLYTEMNESTRA *goes over and shuts all the windows.*

and you can't go out any more
no one must go out
you hear me Electra?
it is important that you listen, that you do what you are told
we are in a new era now
you have to listen to me, we have to do what they tell us
we have to be very careful

CLYTEMNESTRA *goes.*

ELECTRA *is left with the mirror.*

She looks at her reflection again.

She is really itchy.

She starts to scratch.

ELECTRA stop

She shouts into the mirror.

stop stop this

She itches all over.

She smashes the mirror.

Scene Ten

ELECTRA *puts some clothes on.*

She goes in to find the king.

The king is talking to the DOCTOR.

ELECTRA *comes in.*

AEGISTHUS I'm busy

can't you see I am busy?

you walked straight in, you didn't knock

ELECTRA I need to talk to you

AEGISTHUS later

or no, not later, never

do go on Doctor

The DOCTOR *takes a breath to go on but* ELECTRA *hasn't left.*

AEGISTHUS *looks up at her.*

can't you hear properly?

shall I get the doctor to check your ears while he is here?

ELECTRA I want to be sent away

I don't mean just now I mean properly

I want to be sent away far away

That stops the king, he speaks to the DOCTOR.

AEGISTHUS excuse me for a minute

DOCTOR of course

The DOCTOR *retreats a bit.*

The king speaks to ELECTRA.

AEGISTHUS why would you ask to be sent away?

ELECTRA Orestes was sent to school when he was my age

AEGISTHUS Orestes was a boy

ELECTRA there are schools for girls

I want to go to school

AEGISTHUS why on earth out of the blue are you asking to be sent away?

ELECTRA I thought you'd be pleased

AEGISTHUS I might be

if I trusted you

if I didn't think that every single thing you do isn't full of poison

ELECTRA I need an education

at some point I need to learn something

AEGISTHUS you hate me

everything you have done since I have been here has been spiteful, has been to drive a wedge between me and your mother

ELECTRA so send me away

AEGISTHUS this will be some trick

maybe the whole sleep thing was a trick by you

I see it now

somehow you think it will reflect on me

you get sent away and the queen blames me

ah yes that is your game

true to form poison

Doctor have you any way of treating a poisonous girl?

ELECTRA there is nothing wrong with me

AEGISTHUS then stay out of my way.

    keep your evil plans to yourself

    no Electra.

    you asked to go so you must stay

    you must stay here.

    you will stay here and watch your mother become mine.

    if that is what you are trying to avoid, too bad.

    she'll turn away from you and turn towards me.

    that's the right and proper way of these things.

    you watch.

Scene Eleven

ELECTRA *is vomiting.*

No one comes.

She keeps vomiting.

The BUTCHER *eventually comes.*

BUTCHER oh god.

He gets a bucket.

when did this start?

She retches again.

its ok, don't speak.
maybe you should get back to bed

Again she is sick.

it's ok sweetheart
its just a fever or perhaps some bug.
can I have some help in here?

No one answers.

He rubs her back.

ELECTRA it's not a fever

BUTCHER a poison then, maybe you ate something
let's get you back to bed

She seems resistant.

come on if you are sick, it's better to be in bed.

The serving woman, CELIA, *comes in.*

CELIA she'll wake everyone

BUTCHER help me then

CELIA I'm just saying then there'll be all hell to pay
if the king wakes up

BUTCHER wake her mother

CELIA yes that would be for the best
I'll get the queen

ELECTRA *is sick again.*

ELECTRA no not the queen

BUTCHER maybe you got cold today, maybe you picked up a chill

CLYTEMNESTRA *comes in.*

CLYTEMNESTRA what's wrong with her?

BUTCHER she isn't well

CLYTEMNESTRA the smell?
can she smell it too?

CELIA we think she needs her mother

CLYTEMNESTRA but I –
how can I help when I'm like this?
bring a little water, would you
give the girl some water

BUTCHER of course

The **BUTCHER** *goes to get some water.*

ELECTRA *retches again.*

CLYTEMNESTRA *is torn between going to help her and not.*

CLYTEMNESTRA it's ok, it's ok.
you'll be ok

you'll be ok in a bit

oh god

CLYTEMNESTRA *starts to pull away.*

another bucket

CELIA what is it?

CLYTEMNESTRA there are flies in the vomit

CELIA no

CLYTEMNESTRA yes, she is heaving up insects
they are coming out of her mouth

CELIA just some in the bucket perhaps

CLYTEMNESTRA she is turning rotten, I can see it

CELIA nonsense

CLYTEMNESTRA and you, you have dropped something
there must you always be dropping something?

ELECTRA *is sick again.*

everyone everyone is always dropping something
why can people not stop dropping things?

CLYTEMNESTRA *runs off.*

The **BUTCHER** *comes back holding the bucket.*

The serving woman is there too.

Scene Twelve

ELECTRA *and* ORESTES *are outside.* ELECTRA *is sitting on the grass.*

ELECTRA why haven't you gone then?

ORESTES my feet won't take me

simple as that

every day I think I will walk to the next city, I will go in that direction, and every night

ELECTRA that's ridiculous

ORESTES why haven't you gone?

ELECTRA the king won't let me

Beat.

we'll have to leave together.

we could go in the middle of the night

I could pack a bag

ORESTES and go where?

ELECTRA anywhere

ORESTES we'll come back

ELECTRA we could try not to

we have to try not to

ORESTES and scratch for the rest of our lives

ELECTRA what alternative is there?

ORESTES you know what the alternative is

ELECTRA ha ha

ORESTES why are you so loyal to her?

ELECTRA this isn't about loyalty

don't be absurd

ORESTES you and I aren't necessarily the same about everything

ELECTRA Orestes

ORESTES I haven't slept for three weeks

it's ok for you, you still sleep

you wait

in a few weeks you would do anything

there is a dance, the doctors call it a dance when you are so

itchy you go mad

you'll scratch yourself against any tree

people die trying to get rid of an itch

there are times when I want to take my own skin off with a

knife

pour boiling water, anything to make it stop.

Beat.

ELECTRA this is a sort of madness

why is everyone mad?

ORESTES she has convinced you that everything she did, she
did out of love

that she is this perfect woman

ELECTRA she is

ORESTES then why does half the country hate her

have you thought about that?

ELECTRA there are rumours spread

yes ok

ORESTES she killed in cold blood

ELECTRA so did he

ORESTES he thought it was a sex game

she killed him with an erection

Beat.

ELECTRA this is their fight
I don't want to hear about that

ORESTES I'll tell you something about the butcher
I'll tell you something about the pair of them

ELECTRA if this is more lies

ORESTES I met someone who used to work at the palace
someone who fled that night, most people fled that night

ELECTRA the butcher is a good person

ORESTES of course he is

ELECTRA he put me to bed I heard the tale

ORESTES there is a missing patch of that evening
after he cleaned the flagstones
after he put you to bed
no one could find him

ELECTRA so?

ORESTES and no one could find our mother after

ELECTRA I know where they were

ORESTES you heard the tale then?

ELECTRA I know they were with the body
he carried the body

ORESTES but that isn't all

ELECTRA he brought it out to the field

ORESTES he is a butcher
why did she go to the butcher?

Beat.

why did she go to the butcher that night?

Beat.

you know nothing Electra, you know nothing about this
world

ELECTRA I don't want to hear

ORESTES you have to hear

yes this is their fight, but it is also ours

the ghost is making it ours

in the old folk-lore, like they believe in the butcher's town

there is a saying

you want to disempower a ghost

if someone has been murdered say, and you are worried

you do something to the body

ELECTRA I don't believe this

ORESTES why is the butcher so close to her?

they have secrets you know that

ELECTRA stop

ORESTES you want to disempower a ghost, you take a sharp knife

let's say a butche'rs knife and before you bury the body

you cut off the penis

they took off his penis

ELECTRA how do you know?

ORESTES you want to dig him up, check

they took off his penis and they stuck it under his arm

for all of heaven to laugh at

for him for ever to be mocked

you ask anyone

they dug up his body, the men loyal to him

they found his fucking penis under his arm

that is why she is so hated

she used a kind of witchcraft

now I am not saying that she wasn't justified in what she

did

that there wasn't some sense in which

and our sister after all –

but if she was so certain that she was right

why do that to him, he was already dead?

why cut off his penis?

why stick it under his arm?

ELECTRA *sits up.*

ELECTRA that's grotesque

I don't believe you, you fill my head with this stuff

ORESTES she doesn't love you

she doesn't love you

she can't love anyone but herself

it has always been that way

ELECTRA stop it

ORESTES you want me to tell you the tales of when you were
smaller?

she was drunk most of your life

she hardly knew you were there

ELECTRA she was troubled

ORESTES she has always been troubled

when I was a child, before Iphigenia, she was the same

she is a distracted woman

concerned with herself

ELECTRA I won't kill her

ORESTES but let me.

ELECTRA Orestes I can't even believe

ORESTES I can't live like this

I am in torment

give me permission

you and I are the only ones left

Beat.

ELECTRA there is no point asking me, you know what I will say

this is just talk anyway, you

ORESTES then you'll keep me in torment

Beat.

ELECTRA she loves you

ORESTES she is afraid of me

ELECTRA no

ORESTES of course she is, she will have heard the rumours,

that I am the one to avenge

ELECTRA she misses you

ORESTES I bet she never even speaks of me

have you ever heard her bring up my name?

she would like to hear the news that I am dead

that would make her day

if I am dead there is no threat from the ghost

we both know that

ELECTRA you are so wrong

ORESTES I wish I was

ELECTRA let's see then

ORESTES what?

ELECTRA let's tell her you are dead
   see what she does

ORESTES she won't weep

ELECTRA you'll see
   she loves you.

ORESTES and if she doesn't?

ELECTRA if she doesn't weep?

ORESTES yes

ELECTRA Impossible
   she loves her children more than herself, everything she
   does she does for them
   she says that all the time

ORESTES if she doesn't weep?

ELECTRA then yes.
   I'll release you.

Scene Thirteen

ELECTRA *is in the dining room.*

She is setting the scene. Making sure everything is ok.

Putting down a table cloth.

The BUTCHER *comes in. He takes the cloth off her.*

BUTCHER I'll do that

ELECTRA no it's ok

I can do it

Beat.

She sets the cloth.

He starts to move a chair.

I can do that too.

He stops.

BUTCHER is there anything you want from me?

ELECTRA not much.

Beat.

BUTCHER I don't see you now

you used to come to the kitchen and have some milk

ELECTRA I did once

BUTCHER we used to speak sometimes

Beat.

when I pass you in the corridor

ELECTRA I don't have much time

BUTCHER you are changed

ELECTRA do you think you should talk to me like that?

Beat.

BUTCHER what?

ELECTRA I am the one with the title here

you are the butcher

BUTCHER apologies miss.

He looks at her.

ELECTRA go on.

you can go.

He walks out.

ELECTRA *stops. She feels bad.*

She takes a deep breath.

She goes to behind a curtain. **ORESTES** *is there.*

ORESTES that was sharp

ELECTRA he cut off my father's dick, what am I supposed to say?

ORESTES shush someone is coming

ORESTES *pulls back the curtain.*

ELECTRA *sits down.*

Then changes her mind, stands up.

Smoothes her dress down.

Is nervous.

CLYTEMNESTRA *comes in.*

CLYTEMNESTRA I heard there was some news

ELECTRA can you sit down

CLYTEMNESTRA it's news that I need to sit down for?

ELECTRA where's the king?

CLYTEMNESTRA do we need him here too?

ELECTRA how are the flies today?

CLYTEMNESTRA not good.
  worse but the windows are shut

ELECTRA what's that smell?

CLYTEMNESTRA you smell it too

ELECTRA you used to smell like that
  on your breath

CLYTEMNESTRA get away

ELECTRA are you drinking?

CLYTEMNESTRA you told me there was news

  Beat.

ELECTRA Orestes is dead.

  Beat.

CLYTEMNESTRA what?

ELECTRA Orestes is dead.
  Mum, I'm so sorry.

CLYTEMNESTRA how?

ELECTRA I met a man and a woman on the road

CLYTEMNESTRA you went out?

ELECTRA for a short time only

CLYTEMNESTRA what man what woman?

ELECTRA they were on their way to us
  he was on a ship, returning home I think

he had heard about you being asleep
he was coming back to see you

CLYTEMNESTRA how did he die?

ELECTRA he drowned

Beat.

they had a letter explaining what happened
I...

She hands her mother a letter.

CLYTEMNESTRA you read it?

ELECTRA they said it concerned my brother
I thought I could read it, yes I'm sorry –

The queen reads the letter.

CLYTEMNESTRA and it's true?
it's definite?

ELECTRA of course it's true

CLYTEMNESTRA where are this man and this woman?

ELECTRA on the road, we could catch them probably if we

The Queen looks at the letter again.

CLYTEMNESTRA can you call the butcher? The smell is worse
tell him to bring something to take it away
tell the butcher to come quick

She stands up.

oh goodness
oh gods
I...
the flies will break through the window

She looks a little dizzy.

ELECTRA are you ok?

CLYTEMNESTRA my Orestes, my first born
this can't be
my little one
I...
could you bring me some water?
there has been so much death in this house
and get the butcher

ELECTRA *pours her some water.*

CLYTEMNESTRA *sits down and drinks it.*

add something to it would you?
this isn't the time for your disdain
I need a drink my son is dead
I had a dream
a terrifying dream a dream so bad I didn't want to wake up
I dreamt about my Orestes
funny I dreamt about him last night
as a little baby
he was such a lovely baby
not my first of course but
I dreamt he was once again in my arms, his red hair just like
it was the day he was born
a crease across his nose
and I was feeding him
you'll know the joy of feeding a child one day Electra
the close softness
and then as I stroked his little head

I dropped the baby
I dropped him on the floor and instead of it smashing or
crying or
I bent to pick it up
I was scrabbling around trying to pick him up
it turned into a snake and hissed at me
it was a snake I'd had drinking at my breast
not my baby at all
a snake that bit me

She drinks the water.

and now he's dead
according to this letter
I asked a seer
he said it was clear
Orestes would kill me
Orestes was the snake
the flies knew it
I knew it
the gods knew it
Orestes would kill me

She puts the glass back down.

the gods will forgive me I have been frightened yes
I know I am damned
but to be killed by your son

She takes the bottle from the table. Pours it into her glass.

and now you tell me he is drowned.
fuck's sake I need a drink will someone get me something
how can that be?

AEGISTHUS *comes into the room.*

AEGISTHUS what was so urgent I had to be –

CLYTEMNESTRA my son is dead

Orestes, drowned

AEGISTHUS how?

CLYTEMNESTRA returning home it seems

gone, done not far from here

AEGISTHUS *looks to* **ELECTRA.**

a letter came

He takes the letter.

ELECTRA I'm sorry

AEGISTHUS *starts to read the letter.*

CLYTEMNESTRA yes so am I.

very sorry

very very sorry

I'm sorry for you Electra too, you never knew him

AEGISTHUS where were these people?

CLYTEMNESTRA out on the road

AEGISTHUS this is poison

this is some trick

CLYTEMNESTRA no, I can feel it

he is dead

AEGISTHUS well then let's find them, these people that brought
the news

The **BUTCHER** *comes in.*

BUTCHER madam you called

I have made something to clear the smell

CLYTEMNESTRA the smell?

BUTCHER you wanted me to –

She stands up.

CLYTEMNESTRA that's the most surprising thing
the smell has gone

She breathes in.

it's gone
I can't smell anything

The **BUTCHER** *sniffs.*

and the headache

She laughs.

opens the windows, let the outside in
bring me something to celebrate

ELECTRA you must be sad though, your son

CLYTEMNESTRA yes

ELECTRA very sad
maybe you will weep?

CLYTEMNESTRA yes it is sad but
he was young, he had never done anything bad in his life
the gods will look on him favourably
whereas I
if I were to have died
well I am damned
I am not going to die

She laughs.

the seer got it wrong
I am not going to die

She kisses **ELECTRA.**

I think we should celebrate that shouldn't we?

with a drink

She kisses **AEGISTHUS.**

Orestes is dead

I am not going to die

AEGISTHUS *kisses her back.*

AEGISTHUS finally

CLYTEMNESTRA yes finally

She kisses him again.

She laughs.

we can get back to where we should have been.

bring a fucking drink. Let's have a party.

AEGISTHUS *grabs her around the waist and carries her off. She squeals.*

Scene Fourteen

ORESTES *and* **ELECTRA** *are left in the room.*

There is a kind of stunned silence between them.

ORESTES we still don't need to do it

we can spend eternity tormented

it is a suggestion

not a command

the ghost is urging us

we have free will

what are you doing?

ELECTRA I'm listening.

I'm listening to what they are saying as he carries her to
bed.

ORESTES come away

Beat.

ELECTRA I always knew she wasn't exactly

well no one is perfect

is anyone perfect?

I knew she would forget me sometimes

and sometimes she would say she would come up and then

wouldn't

or even some times she wouldn't see me at all for days

leave me waiting

and when she was drinking of course

but I always thought

that somewhere

sometime

the next time

deep down that really

ORESTES we don't have to do this

ELECTRA you were right about her

ORESTES I think we should think about

ELECTRA rip down the walls

see what they are doing in there

ORESTES it is natural

ELECTRA you should have stood at the wall and listened to what they said as they walked away

you have to have good ears if you want to know what goes on in here

he knew the letter was false, I could see that

he knew that there was no woman and no man on the road

you see he didn't send anyone to find them

he's clever, he knew

he says I am full of poison, maybe I am

ORESTES what did he say?

ELECTRA he told her

he said, Orestes isn't dead this is a false report

ORESTES I didn't hear that

ELECTRA but I did

you didn't stand where I stood

ORESTES and what did she say?

ELECTRA she said the thing that damns her most of all.

she said, then find him then and kill him.

Beat.

ELECTRA *looks at* ORESTES.

she said find him then and kill him

kill my son

ORESTES you misheard

ELECTRA I didn't.

you were right about her.

you were right, how can you say I misheard?

you were right.

CLYTEMNESTRA *comes in, half dressed, to get the bottle.*

CLYTEMNESTRA oh, I am sorry Electra I didn't realize

AEGISTHUS*'s voice off.*

AEGISTHUS hurry darling

CLYTEMNESTRA I will I just

who's this?

ORESTES *gets out a knife.*

ORESTES I'm your son mother

CLYTEMNESTRA but

ORESTES it's been so long you don't even recognize me

CLYTEMNESTRA of course I recognize you

Aegisthus

ORESTES don't call for anyone

CLYTEMNESTRA now wait a minute, don't come near me

put that away

ORESTES this is not from me, this is from my father

CLYTEMNESTRA Orestes, no

ELECTRA *drops the thing she is holding.*

It smashes.

ORESTES *grabs his mother, gets her into a hold.*

He doesn't kill her though straight away, hesitates, panics.

you don't have the nerve,

you always were a timid boy

you can't do this

ORESTES don't push me

CLYTEMNESTRA do it then

ORESTES I...

He drops the knife.

CLYTEMNESTRA you can't kill your mother

you see?

it's against the law of nature

ELECTRA *comes over.*

She picks up the knife.

tell him Electra

there's no one that loves you more than a mother

no one that loves her children more than a mother does.

ELECTRA *puts the knife into* **CLYTEMNESTRA.**

CLYTEMNESTRA *falls.*

She is screaming.

ORESTES finish her, you only half did it

ELECTRA you do it

ORESTES I can't.

ELECTRA *puts it into her again. Cold-blooded.*

The screaming stops.

AEGISTHUS *comes in, half dressed.*

AEGISTHUS oh god
what the hell – guards
you're surrounded

ORESTES by who?

AEGISTHUS you won't get away with this

ORESTES everyone hates you more than we do

ORESTES *grabs him, they fight.*

AEGISTHUS someone will stop you, someone will
you think you have strength

ORESTES *kills him swiftly. He breaks his neck.*

AEGISTHUS *falls down on the floor.*

Silence.

ORESTES *and* ELECTRA *look at what they have done.*

They are covered in blood.

They look at each other.

ORESTES ok?

ELECTRA yes ok.

ORESTES sure?

ELECTRA sure

The BUTCHER *comes running in.*

BUTCHER what's the noise?

what's going on what is going on here?

He sees the two bodies.

what?

what have you done?

oh hell.

what have you done?

CELIA *is behind him.*

She sees the bodies too, and puts her hand to her face.

ELECTRA there is nothing here for you, please leave us

The BUTCHER *runs to the Queen.*

ORESTES *takes the knife from* ELECTRA, *he uses the table
cloth to wipe it.*

BUTCHER maybe she isn't dead, maybe if we stop the bleeding

re-start the heart. Help –

ELECTRA there is no one here

who will hear you?

BUTCHER the doctor, someone call the doctor

he isn't far

what have you done you evil girl?

The woman pulls him away from the Queen's body.

CELIA she's dead

they both are

you have to come away

BUTCHER but these two

CELIA nothing can be done

this time you have to run

BUTCHER Electra, this isn't you

CELIA the curse on this house is too much

you warned me that the curse here

BUTCHER Electra –

CELIA you can't wash the flagstones again, try to solve it

you can't keep washing the flagstones

not again

BUTCHER Electra – look at me

CELIA come with me now

She pulls him away.

come on, it's time to leave this.

CELIA *and the* **BUTCHER** *leave.*

ORESTES *and* **ELECTRA** *are left.*

ORESTES *wipes the blood from* **ELECTRA***'s face.*

Carefully. Tenderly.

ORESTES the curse is broken

ELECTRA the itch?

ORESTES gone

everything that was done between them

it's over now

ELECTRA yes

ORESTES we're free then? Aren't we?

we can do what we want with our lives

live differently

we'll bury them

we will put all three in a proper grave

it finishes here
the woman was right this has been a curse
a curse that goes back as long as either of us can remember
but now

ELECTRA'*s hand starts to shake.*

what is that with your hand?

ELECTRA I don't know it

ORESTES just the shock

ELECTRA yes

ORESTES let's go to the kitchen and get you something sweet
everyone will have gone, we'll have the place to ourselves

Her hand shakes even more.

what is it?

ELECTRA I don't know

She looks at her arms, her legs.

She can't control it.

what's happening to me?

ORESTES *tries to hold her.*

ORESTES it'll be ok, just try to take some deep breaths

ELECTRA help me

The shakes take over her whole body.

Then she falls to the floor. This is a full-blown seizure.

ORESTES stop if you can Electra

ELECTRA deep breaths

ORESTES *calls out to anyone that will listen.*

help

out there

someone help

someone help my sister

someone help my sister please

ELECTRA *continues to shake.*

someone help my sister.

ELECTRA AND HER SHADOW

Scene One

ELECTRA *is holding the knife exactly the same as at the end of the previous play.*

She is shaking.

She is otherwise alone on stage.

ELECTRA Orestes?

Orestes are you there?

don't piss about –

Orestes?

is that you?

I can hear you

She moves around the stage with the knife.

if you're playing a game

then fuck off, fuck off with your teasing

There is a sniffing.

A snuffling, an odd sort of noise. Unsettling. It's not even clear where it comes from.

this isn't funny

don't scare me

Face-less forms seem to be in the shadows, or is it her imagination?

There is a chill, a wind.

stop it, Orestes.

She looks around.

Orestes. Stop it.

stop it.

She is in the middle of a wood.

She looks around.

CLYTEMNESTRA *is sitting in a chair. Blood all down her.*

CLYTEMNESTRA hell my darling
I could see your mouth moving to ask the question
hell is the answer

ELECTRA that can't be you –

CLYTEMNESTRA yes me

ELECTRA *looks around.*

ELECTRA but, how can it be? I just

CLYTEMNESTRA put a knife through me?
well done but now

ELECTRA you're alive?

CLYTEMNESTRA sadly not
very dead and this place...

ELECTRA where's Orestes?

CLYTEMNESTRA gone
the palace gone
everything you know, gone
you know of all my kids I expected this least from you
you were my little biddable poppet

ELECTRA stay away from me

CLYTEMNESTRA I can't even touch you

you might not like being here but look Electra

at least look at me

CLYTEMNESTRA if you wish

ELECTRA get back

ELECTRA *backs away.*

CLYTEMNESTRA oh sweetheart there is a lot worse to come

you have unleashed something

ELECTRA what do you mean?

CLYTEMNESTRA I don't know but can't you hear them?

scratching, sniffing

in the dark when you have your eyes shut

moving about in the undergrowth

ELECTRA I'm not scared

CLYTEMNESTRA you should be

you should be very very scared

you killed your mother. You foolish girl

all hell is coming for you now

you had better run

The sound returns, terrible now. And terrifying.

All around. ELECTRA *doesn't know which way to turn.*

The lights change. ELECTRA *is on a snow-covered mountain.*

ELECTRA oh god

Her dad is standing beside her, she doesn't see him at first.

AGAMEMNON Electra

ELECTRA please Mum if that's you

AGAMEMNON my baby

ELECTRA what?

AGAMEMNON it's me your father

ELECTRA *looks at him for the first time.*

ELECTRA my father's dead

AGAMEMNON yes ok, but here to help you
you have to fight this, you can't let them destroy you

ELECTRA what are they?

AGAMEMNON I don't know but your mother is behind it
take everything I have, all the power I had
you just have to find their weakness
if they are sent by your mother then they'll have a weakness
arm yourself, find every weapon you can
think like a soldier you have to fight back

ELECTRA *hears the wind again.*

ELECTRA I don't even know which direction they are coming
from

AGAMEMNON it's the blood on your hands
that's what is bringing them

She looks down.

She wipes her hands.

ELECTRA there's blood on us both

AGAMEMNON but my crimes do not insult them like yours

ELECTRA I can't fight

AGAMEMNON then keep the window shut

don't let them in

if you can't fight them, keep them out

ELECTRA what window?

The noise starts to come back.

DAD?

She looks about her.

AGAMEMNON run Electra

ELECTRA DAD?

AGAMEMNON run

He has gone.

She is on a beach.

She sits up.

ELECTRA where now?

ORESTES don't ask

ELECTRA Orestes? Thank god

we have to get out of here

ORESTES I wish it was different –

ELECTRA what was different?

ORESTES I am not with you any more

ELECTRA yes you were in the palace beside me

something terrible is after us

ORESTES I was yes, right by your side

but then

ELECTRA no don't tell me

ORESTES we were in the dining room

ELECTRA on the floor

ORESTES you started shaking
　　this terrible shaking,
　　Electra I was scared
　　forgive me please, when I saw what had happened to you

ELECTRA forgive you?

ORESTES I went into a panic
　　I knew the gods were angry

ELECTRA there are no gods

ORESTES ok creatures older than the gods even
　　these terrors and spirits
　　I heard them
　　I ran out into the field and with a piece of rope

ELECTRA no

ORESTES we broke some rule
　　I'm sorry Electra
　　when I saw them coming

ELECTRA we're together, we're together in this

ORESTES not any more
　　it was your hand holding the knife
　　it's you they want

ELECTRA you left me

ORESTES I'm no use to you, I never was any use

ELECTRA so be of use now, how do I face this?

ORESTES I don't know what the answer is
　　I think you should run

ELECTRA where to?

ORESTES who knows?
　　a place they won't find you

ELECTRA and where is that?

where the hell is that?

where do I run?

The CHORUS *come on to stage.*

They sing a song. A song about a woman that runs around the whole world. A woman that never stops running. It's a sort of lullaby, but then gets fucked up. One of them keeps fucking it up. The CHORUS *get cross with each other.* CLYTEMNESTRA *says she knows this one and joins in. She picks up the story about the woman that ran, it has become scatological. She forgets the rhyme that goes at the end of it.* AGAMEMNON *and* ORESTES *join in with the* CHORUS. *They take a turn. They seem more modern now. Microphones and guitars. One of them is still trying to keep it sweet. What hope for a good ending is there? Does anyone know?*

ELECTRA *even has a solo spot.*

When it comes to her verse, the answer about is there any hope of a happy ending, she has the microphone. She answers.

None at all.

Scene Two

AUDREY *enters carrying a whole load of files.*

She goes over to the filing cabinet. She puts the files in the filing cabinet.

She speaks to a CHORUS *member that is in her way.*

AUDREY you shouldn't be here

and I know you are listening because your hand twitches

when you are off in a dwam

Jordan, should you be here?

JORDAN *looks confused.*

JORDAN I think I...

AUDREY exactly.

back out the door, along the corridor

go and sit in the day room

do you want me to ring for the nurse?

AUDREY *puts the files back, ignoring him.*

He still stands there.

She takes down a sweetie jar.

alright, one. Then back to your ward

She opens it, she gives him one.

JORDAN *sucks on the sweet and goes out.*

As he goes he passes MICHAEL *on the way in.*

MICHAEL I thought you didn't do that any more

AUDREY it's Jordan

MICHAEL new paper out, shouldn't reward

AUDREY again, it's Jordan

MICHAEL they're all somebody

AUDREY sweet tooth

MICHAEL you brought magazines in for Carol

don't tell me, it's Carol

and special pyjamas for Ted

AUDREY what can I say?

busted.

Beat.

life is miserable enough, isn't it?

the odd sweet

MICHAEL quite but who is going to do that when you have gone?

AUDREY if you've come to try and talk me out of going

MICHAEL heaven forfend. I know when a mind is made up

besides isn't it too late?

AUDREY you could say

could you move over actually? I have to get into that drawer

MICHAEL sorry

He moves a bit. Not enough.

are you sorting it all already?

AUDREY I've got to make a start

you wouldn't believe the amount of crap I have accrued

the case notes are the tip of the iceberg, and most of them

should be on computer

He is still in the way.

can you budge a bit more?

He moves a bit more. An exasperatingly small amount.

not in a clinic?

MICHAEL finished early

AUDREY oh.

He is completely in the way, he moves off the filing cabinet.

MICHAEL Judy says come over to the house, we'll have a meal before you go

AUDREY that would be nice.

Beat.

He stops and looks at her.

She looks at him.

don't

MICHAEL I know.

I won't. But

Beat.

you are the only one that agrees with me around here

once you have gone

AUDREY then get out yourself

MICHAEL where?

it's alright for you, at your time of life

AUDREY Keith won't be here for ever

MICHAEL I don't want to run the department

that's a whole other ball game

all the petty politics

AUDREY maybe they'll give you a job in Ohio

MICHAEL I doubt it

and anyway I'd never move Judy

Beat.

it's not just about the job, or Jordan and his sweets

I'll miss you

AUDREY I know

I'll miss you too

this building though I won't miss

apparently I get a view right across the river in my next

office

MICHAEL do you want a drink?

AUDREY I've got patients to see

MICHAEL alright. Later. Sorry I have been so morose

up-beat next time, I promise

you know you've got your window open

AUDREY oh?

MICHAEL shall I shut it?

AUDREY I don't remember opening it

MICHAEL well it's open now

easy fixed

He shuts it.

AUDREY *looks at the window.*

AUDREY perhaps Jordan opened it.

AUDREY *goes over and makes sure it is shut.*

MICHAEL have a drink with me

> you are a bloody good psychiatrist, you can do it on half a
> glass of sherry

AUDREY you'll be fine without me

MICHAEL practically your final clinic anyway

> come on

AUDREY you won't miss me

MICHAEL there is no other voice of sense

AUDREY I need a sharp head

MICHAEL do you think you might be too meticulous?

AUDREY often

MICHAEL too bloody perfect?

AUDREY careful.

MICHAEL I think I might love you

AUDREY fuck off.

> alright

> AUDREY *gets a bottle of sherry out of a filing cabinet.*

> *She pours them both a glass.*

> a quick one. I get a view across the river in Ohio

MICHAEL you said

AUDREY better weather

> less patients

> more pay

MICHAEL are you trying to make me even more miserable?

AUDREY remember the week you started

MICHAEL how could I not?

AUDREY the look on your face as I walked in

MICHAEL it was a surprise.

    I can say that

AUDREY for us both

MICHAEL I'm sure

    you see people as patients

    they come they go, you never see them again

    or they never leave

    they don't turn up fully intact

AUDREY I didn't expect to see you either

    fifteen years

MICHAEL I know

    and a name change

AUDREY anyway it worked out

    didn't it?

MICHAEL so far

AUDREY bugger off

    They laugh slightly.

    cheers

    They drink.

MICHAEL saw you saw some of your old patients again yesterday

AUDREY I put some of them down for my clinic, yes

    I had space

MICHAEL how did it go?

AUDREY fine

MICHAEL ok

AUDREY why are you asking?

MICHAEL no reason

AUDREY you never normally ask about my clinics

MICHAEL we never normally have a drink in the afternoon
is there a problem with that?

AUDREY the drink or the asking?

Beat.

MICHAEL I was just surprised that is all
to see you go back to your old list

AUDREY I wanted to say goodbye to this place
to them

MICHAEL other people look after that ward now

AUDREY so there is a problem

MICHAEL Audrey no
you're a grown-up
you're a bloody good psychiatrist as I said.

Beat.

AUDREY there are some loose ends

MICHAEL be careful

AUDREY you cured me

MICHAEL I know I did

Beat.

AUDREY I'm only here for another three weeks
yes there is a kind of black mark
most people respond to something, in the end
or they just get so much worse that they disappear and the
body gives up
but

MICHAEL some people we can't help

AUDREY I am only here for another three weeks

is there is such a danger in trying?

MICHAEL your window is open again

AUDREY what?

She looks.

no it isn't

MICHAEL but you jumped. You looked in alarm

AUDREY for god's sake

MICHAEL I was the person who went through it with you

you're jumpy

AUDREY the window opened today because, I don't know why the

window was open

maybe I opened it and I forgot

or Jordan or

what the fuck are you doing playing games with me?

MICHAEL I'm sorry you are reacting like this

AUDREY she was a patient of mine for a long time

I have three weeks before I go.

if I can do something

stop looking at the fucking window

MICHAEL I've made you cross

AUDREY damn right you have

Beat.

He hands his glass back to her.

MICHAEL I'm sorry

she and you weren't the same

your cases are different

AUDREY I know.

MICHAEL enjoy the last three weeks here Audrey.

you're such a valuable member of our team

so loved

don't let her drag you back to somewhere.

AUDREY how could she?

MICHAEL indeed.

how could she?

A psychiatric nurse, **MEGAN,** *comes in.*

MEGAN that's your clinic starting Audrey

AUDREY thank you

MEGAN some have been waiting a little while, what shall I tell them?

AUDREY I'm coming

AUDREY *picks up some files and walks out in a rush.*

MEGAN *is left with* **MICHAEL.** *She sees the glasses of sherry.*

MEGAN didn't know this was a party

MICHAEL it wasn't

Scene Three

ELECTRA *sits in a chair.*

AUDREY *stands a little way off.*

ELECTRA you stopped seeing me

AUDREY doctors move on, we see a patient for a while we feel we aren't getting anywhere

ELECTRA you passed me on

Beat.

AUDREY it became complicated

ELECTRA so why are you back?

AUDREY I...

you're a curiosity around here

you don't fit, you know that

most of the patients, well there is a thing that goes with mental illness

ELECTRA I'm not mentally ill

AUDREY that isn't actually the complication, many people with symptoms say that but you – most people's symptoms can be medicated in the end, the doses might get high and get sleepy but the psychosis is suppressed.

You – we give higher and higher doses of medication, neither does it have any effect nor does it appear to sedate you

ELECTRA that is because it isn't psychosis

AUDREY of course

ELECTRA if it was psychosis I would respond

AUDREY indeed

not psychosis then, a sort of paranoia, a high state of anxiety and terror that nothing seems to relieve

ELECTRA I am cursed

AUDREY and you know I have heard your explanation

ELECTRA but you don't believe it

AUDREY we are here to explore the connection between the psyche and the body, the physical manifestations of your belief that you are being hunted

ELECTRA I am

AUDREY and I promise we will explore that

ELECTRA hell will get me one day.

AUDREY not if I can help it

ELECTRA the window isn't even shut properly. You haven't put the bolt across. The door could swing open at any second.

there are cracks in the floorboards. There is a vent through which anything could come

AUDREY *stands up.*

AUDREY I can put a bolt across the window

I will do whatever I can to make you feel safe

ELECTRA I never feel safe

AUDREY *looks at the vent.*

AUDREY I hadn't noticed the vent

ELECTRA and there is an old chimney behind that wall.

AUDREY *stands on a chair.*

AUDREY I'll ask them to look into that

ELECTRA the nurses don't check under the beds properly.

there are little holes in the skirting boards

AUDREY we can fill the holes

ELECTRA if you restrain me I can't even run

AUDREY you were running for years

it did you no good

ELECTRA just let me go

ELECTRA *pulls at the restraints.*

please

AUDREY your clothes had fallen away

you were so dehydrated you were nearly dead

ELECTRA what else is there to do?

Beat.

ELECTRA *pulls again at the ties holding her.*

AUDREY you know if you took responsibility for what you did,
then release might be –

ELECTRA I have taken responsibility

AUDREY metabolized your remorse

ELECTRA how can I be remorseful for something I was supposed
to do?

AUDREY you understand you killed your mother

ELECTRA of course I do

but she deserved to die

AUDREY *rubs her face in her hands.*

AUDREY I think this is where you get blocked

I think this is the root of it all

ELECTRA it wasn't just a voice in my head, it wasn't just a
feeling of compulsion

she was going to kill my brother

AUDREY what literally, in front of you?

ELECTRA she killed my father, she is capable of anything

AUDREY you understand the theories of how the mind works,
don't you? You've read the books I lent you

ELECTRA she sent them to hunt me

AUDREY Klein's *Love, Guilt and Separation*

ELECTRA they are a curse from her

AUDREY she is dead

ELECTRA yes but even dead

you watching now Mum, you enjoying this?

AUDREY there is this fixation on your mother

ELECTRA because she's enjoying it, and it isn't fair

There is a noise.

AUDREY that is just the air conditioning

no need for your alarm, it's a new system

AUDREY *stands up, looks at the vent.*

I'll get someone to check it

She comes back down, sits on the chair.

ELECTRA you can't take your eye off the little spaces, they can
crawl through anything, wherever there is a gap

I ask my father, there must be someone I can appeal to

even hell must have some sort of reason.

AUDREY and what does he say?

ELECTRA my father is useless

he says I should wrap a piece of ribbon around my wrist

and then there is my brother

AUDREY you see all your family?

ELECTRA I see everyone

the whole household, pretty much everywhere

Beat.

AUDREY *looks at her.*

you are making a note

AUDREY I am thinking.

ELECTRA you'll say something clever and this will all be over?

AUDREY I doubt it.

ELECTRA then what's the point?

Beat.

AUDREY you're an intelligent person Electra

you know you're in a permanent state of terror and

paranoia brought on by your crime

that is the diagnosis, the worst anyone has ever seen when

you have an attack

and distressing of course

but tell me

if they are so powerful is a window enough? A door, a bolt,

the nurse checking the spaces

ELECTRA why do you say that?

AUDREY put it another way, they want you

they are coming for you

you say you are being hunted, wrongly

ELECTRA they do come in sometimes

they come in and play sometimes

AUDREY tell me about that

ELECTRA they are the spirit of the torture chamber

the executioners' knife

there is no pain like it

so painful that you forget who you are

and just when I can bear no more, and I am crying out,

they whisper or laugh in my ear

they say they will be back another day and then it will be worse

Beat.

AUDREY I didn't realise they could talk?

ELECTRA I can hear what they are saying, yes

Beat.

AUDREY when we have these episodes on tape, and it looks like you bruise yourself

ELECTRA they bruise me

AUDREY you can see why it is difficult for us to understand

ELECTRA they bite and kick and rip then leave me healed so they can do it again

AUDREY I see

Beat.

ELECTRA I have a message actually

Beat.

the message is for you

AUDREY ok

ELECTRA when they came the time before, they whispered something

AUDREY what did they whisper?

ELECTRA they whispered that they are coming for you too.

Beat.

AUDREY right I see

ELECTRA they've been hunting for you as well

you don't have to believe me

AUDREY are you trying to scare me too, so we can sit in the same place?

ELECTRA I'm just passing on a message

AUDREY from them?

ELECTRA yes from them

AUDREY well thank you for the message

ELECTRA I think you knew that already

AUDREY if they come for me, I will deal with it.

Beat.

ELECTRA you had better be prepared

AUDREY I will be

ELECTRA they are no fun

Beat.

is it my time?

AUDREY yes

that is your time.

thank you Electra.

I'll get a nurse to take you back.

Scene Four

AUDREY *goes in to see* MICHAEL *in his office.*

MICHAEL long day?

AUDREY aren't they all?

MICHAEL I'm up to my ears in it, Lesley W's back

AUDREY I thought she was discharged

MICHAEL well she returned

could you sign this?

right royal mess, we shouldn't have discharged her in the community's view

read it first

AUDREY do I want to?

MICHAEL no, probably not

you're out of here after all.

sign if you could,

AUDREY *signs.*

what did you want?

AUDREY not sure

MICHAEL you going for a run?

AUDREY I was thinking about it, how can you tell?

MICHAEL you're holding your trainers

AUDREY *looks down.*

AUDREY oh

need to clear my head

running is good for that

MICHAEL wish I was as disciplined, could do with getting rid of some of this spare –

AUDREY hallucinations, gremlins what are they?

MICHAEL what?

AUDREY what sort of thing?

MICHAEL what sort of thing are hallucinations?

AUDREY yes

MICHAEL sensory reworkings often

AUDREY of what?

MICHAEL past experiences
  memories, desires
  emotions
  dreams sometimes

AUDREY anything else?

MICHAEL internal states, you know the range is enormous
  you just about wrote the book on these things, why are you
  asking me?

AUDREY I'm just checking

  She puts her shoes on.

  internal states absolutely. Guilt being one of the most
  painful to the ego
  that we didn't act as we wished we had, because it
  contradicts who we think we should be, who we are
  it's an irritant
  or we feel we were wronged, that we shouldn't be blamed
  that the universe is unjust
  and that is always it, there is never anything else

MICHAEL is everything ok?

AUDREY of course it is

  She does her shoelaces up.

damn

The lace snaps.

MICHAEL what?

AUDREY the bloody lace, that's all nothing
I did it too tight

MICHAEL let me see
what's wrong with your finger?

AUDREY*'s finger is bleeding.*

AUDREY I caught it

MICHAEL on the lace?

AUDREY it's ok, I'll go for a run later

MICHAEL the shoes look knackered

AUDREY no, they're new

MICHAEL they look like they have run a fair while already

He picks them up.

let me
soles all worn

AUDREY I bought them last week

MICHAEL then get a refund

She takes them back.

She looks at the soles.

She looks at the blood on her finger.

The window flies up.

AUDREY shut the bloody window would you?

MICHAEL *looks at her.*

Scene Five

AUDREY *puts her shoes on the table.*

She and ELECTRA *are on either side.*

AUDREY *shows her the shoes.*

AUDREY how did you know?

ELECTRA I didn't know

AUDREY when you said you had a message for me, I think you knew the effect it would have

ELECTRA not at all

AUDREY stop playing games with me

ELECTRA I'm not

Beat.

AUDREY these are new trainers, I bought them last week.

I haven't even used them but the soles are all worn

ELECTRA ok?

AUDREY I have been running in my sleep. It's obvious I have been running in my sleep, you know I have been running in my sleep, you seem to know everything now either I have been running in my sleep generally or I have been running in my sleep after seeing you again

it means nothing that I have been running in my sleep

how did you know I was running in my sleep?

ELECTRA did they come after you?

AUDREY of course they didn't Electra because there is no them

that is what I have spent my life dedicated to proving

there is no them

there is only us

everything that we believe is external
is internal
it's a re-working of a painful emotion
in your case guilt

ELECTRA and in yours

AUDREY my case is different

ELECTRA they said your father's name was Ian

AUDREY you know nothing about me

ELECTRA he's sent them to you like my mother sent them to me

AUDREY there are no gods no gremlins, no curses
the whole of modern medicine proves that

ELECTRA why don't you do the talking?

AUDREY stop this, just bloody well stop this.

Beat.

AUDREY *gets herself together.*

listen I am not going to play games with you
people can get a thing about their therapists
it happens often
we are trained to work around it
it is a part of the process
projection
you can project on to the therapist, the good bits, the bad
bits, the bits that are too complicated, you can treat them
like your mother for a bit, your father
your bloody abuser, your good side, your bad side, the
therapist can be anyone
but I am not in this with you
I am not being hunted

do you understand that?

they are hunting you not me

ELECTRA you admit it then, I'm being hunted

Beat.

AUDREY of course you aren't

ELECTRA you just said

AUDREY a slip of the tongue

ELECTRA then why are you sweating?

AUDREY you are not improving

I was warned against seeing you again

we did this before, we moved on

it is only because I am starting a new job that I thought it

would be clean, nice to see how you were

you were doing well with Dr Conway, I'll suggest you go

back to him

you and I, I shouldn't have seen you again

ELECTRA either I am crazy, or they really are coming

AUDREY you're crazy

ELECTRA you don't think I am

that is why I bother you so much

that is why I bother you all

AUDREY you are a dangerous mind

ELECTRA listen

AUDREY that's the air conditioning

Electra I don't want to have to call for a nurse

ELECTRA the window is open

AUDREY I'll shut it

ELECTRA don't shut it for me

shut it for you

AUDREY there is no need to shut if for me but because I can see the distress you are in, I will shut it for you

you are right, there is a memo on your notes saying the window should be shut at all times

AUDREY *goes over and shuts it.*

it's shut now, I'll get the nurse to call you back to your room

Scene Six

AUDREY *is by the sinks, washing her hands.*

She looks at her hands.

There is nothing wrong with her hands.

She looks at the soles of her shoes.

JORDAN *comes in.*

AUDREY you shouldn't be in here

JORDAN I followed you in because you looked upset

AUDREY this is the ladies' toilet Jordan

JORDAN if anyone hurts you, you know I'd do them

AUDREY you should go back to the day room

JORDAN what's wrong with your shoes?

AUDREY nothing

JORDAN you are the best you know.

the best there is,

we all say it

there is nothing you wouldn't do for someone

AUDREY thank you Jordan.

JORDAN you got a sweet?

AUDREY I'll bring you one later.

JORDAN *goes. Fuck it, she thinks.*

Scene Seven

ELECTRA *is in her room.*

ORESTES *is on a swing.*

ORESTES I was never any good to you

ELECTRA too right there

ORESTES I hate myself for leaving you

ELECTRA you could have brought a fucking piece of rope for me
that is what you could have done
that is what most people would have done

ORESTES you'll upset yourself

ELECTRA so fucking what, so I upset myself?
maybe I need to get really fucking upset for once
maybe I need you to know how bloody screwed I am
I can't run, I can't sit still, I can't escape
I can't end it
I am on my own
if there is a god up there, bloody help me

ORESTES oh fuck

ELECTRA *looks at him.*

some fucker left the window open

ELECTRA what?

ELECTRA *looks.*

ELECTRA *pulls on a bell.*

The window flies up.

The winds outside howl.

the window

someone please get the window

ELECTRA *tries to stand up. She is chained to the bed.*

She can't get far, she is straining to get away from the window.

can anyone hear me?

the window is open

All around her is sniffing.

JORDAN *comes in.*

Jordan please

get some help, the window

JORDAN *wanders off.*

Others are watching but are also useless.

someone

The sniffing gets louder.

no, stay away

She tries to shut the window.

Her restraints stop her.

She can't get to it.

Orestes are you still there?

A nurse comes in.

ELECTRA *struggles.*

the window

The nurse rings for someone else.

MEGAN there is nothing wrong with the window

ELECTRA shut it

MEGAN you need air

ELECTRA no please

The sniffing and howling comes from all sides. Like a tidal wave.

MEGAN bite down on this Electra

ELECTRA but I can't

MEGAN I need some help in here, some preparation

ELECTRA please just

She is starting to thrash about.

get them away from me

A second nurse comes in.

The **CHORUS** *come and watch.*

ELECTRA *is surrounded by an imaginary pack of dogs.*

you'll rip me, you'll

They are barking at her.

Twisting her.

ELECTRA *tries to fight them, struggling this way and that.*

Two nurses and a doctor come in.

They get **ELECTRA** *into a restraint position.*

She is struggling around, trying to get out.

The dog noises change to laughter.

There is laughter all around.

ELECTRA *rails at that too.*

no don't laugh at me

The nurses speak to her.

MEGAN no one is laughing at you Electra

CLYTEMNESTRA's *face seems like it is everywhere.*

The laughing gets louder and louder.

ELECTRA if there is a god, please end this

god are you there?

ELECTRA *is given an electric shock. From all sides and suddenly.*

The world goes black.

Scene Eight

MICHAEL *and* AUDREY *look at* ELECTRA. *Asleep.*

AUDREY she shouldn't have been given that

MICHAEL we've had good results with electric shock therapy
before

AUDREY not with her, it didn't work with her

MICHAEL we had nothing else to try

AUDREY she is my patient

MICHAEL not technically

AUDREY we agreed we wouldn't with her again

MICHAEL let's face it, some people

AUDREY one of the nurses left the window open

MICHAEL so?

Beat.

AUDREY it scares her
scared her
if she woke and the window was open
maybe it was our fault
there's a note that the window should never be open in her
room, I think that should be looked into

MICHAEL oh you mean it is her own fear that causes this?

AUDREY yes of course

MICHAEL because it sounded for a moment like you thought
it was the window

AUDREY don't be daft

MICHAEL you won't mind my opening the window now then

AUDREY but she

MICHAEL she's asleep

the electric shock we dispensed was so powerful that it did eventually cause enough of an neurological crisis for the brain to shut down

Beat.

if it is her own fear and she is asleep

this room is a little stuffy, I think we could all do with some air

AUDREY ok sure

MICHAEL ok

MICHAEL *starts to walk towards the window.*

AUDREY don't

MICHAEL Audrey

AUDREY she had a bad night, can't we leave it at that?

MICHAEL not until you open the window

AUDREY I'm not frightened of anything

MICHAEL like hell you aren't

AUDREY you don't know anything

MICHAEL so open the window

Beat.

I know a grown woman, a top brain, someone destined to be a leader in her field won't open a window

that's what I know.

AUDREY I will open it

MICHAEL then go ahead

AUDREY *goes over to it.*

She opens it.

Nothing happens.

AUDREY there you see, open

MICHAEL good

AUDREY you'll leave me alone now?

She shuts it again.

MICHAEL why not leave it open?

AUDREY it's cold

MICHAEL it's the middle of summer

hot I would say

She opens it again.

Just a little.

we went through this at the time

there is no such thing as a curse

AUDREY have you actually got a reason to be in here?

MICHAEL we all have patients we can't cure, people who are too like ourselves

AUDREY only this isn't either of our offices and I don't think this conversation

MICHAEL Alright

but she is like your shadow, and you need to let her go.

He goes.

Scene Nine

Later, AUDREY *is on her own.*

She is in front of the window.

She opens it.

Nothing happens.

She shuts it again.

She takes a deep breath.

She opens it.

Nothing.

Then a sniffing sound.

She listens.

She shuts it.

Song from the CHORUS.

CHORUS
THE CRACKS IN THE WINDOW. THE CRACKS IN THE GLASS.
    THE CRACKS IN THE CEILING, THE CRACKS IN THE HOUSE.
THE CRACKS IN THE FACE THAT CAN'T BE PUT ON IN THE
    MORNING.
THE CRACKS IN THE WOMEN WHO ARE FALLING APART.

Scene Ten

AUDREY *and* ELECTRA.

ELECTRA *is talking now.*

AUDREY *is in the wood, and* ELECTRA *is at the side narrating what happens as.*

AUDREY you are in a wood

ELECTRA yes

AUDREY and she is in front of you

ELECTRA to one side

AUDREY yes ok to one side
always in the same place?

ELECTRA pretty much

AUDREY she looks like she is smiling, laughing

AUDREY *can see* CLYTEMNESTRA *is front of her.*

ELECTRA well not laughing sort of
it's hard to tell
when I'm there the pain

AUDREY a physical pain?

ELECTRA above the ribs, but sort of spreading out across the back

AUDREY as if you feel her wounds
does she talk?

ELECTRA sometimes, sometimes she just looks at me
I see her bleeding

AUDREY do you feel anything?

ELECTRA I hear the sniffing, the noises from them

AUDREY where from?

ELECTRA behind

> she says they will hunt me

AUDREY and it's her that sends them, you're sure?

ELECTRA it isn't guilt

AUDREY I'm not saying it is anything I am just asking the question.

> I have to ask questions Electra, that is my job.

ELECTRA next I'm on a mountain

> there was a mountain that we used to go to. I'm there with my father.

AUDREY ok, we're on a mountain

ELECTRA I never really met my father, but somehow

AUDREY where is he in relation to you?

> physically

ELECTRA in front of me

AUDREY ah I see

> dressed, always the same?

ELECTRA in his armour

> I guess that doesn't make sense either
>
> he was killed in the nude

AUDREY it's not supposed to make sense, go on

ELECTRA he's angry, about Mum. He's shouting saying I have to this and that, fight and avenge. He says she was always evil, he gives me a ribbon from his wrist

AUDREY a ribbon?

ELECTRA yes, always the same

> **AGAMEMNON** *gives a ribbon to* **AUDREY**.

> it's supposed to keep evil spirits away

AUDREY and does it?

ELECTRA obviously not.

AUDREY *takes the ribbon.*

She looks at it.

Beat.

It's not a ribbon, it's a bouncy ball. She drops it.

She stumbles slightly.

can we go on?

AUDREY yes. I just
are you sure it's a ribbon?

ELECTRA yep

AUDREY and always blue?

*She stands out and pours herself a glass of water from
a jug.*

just a moment

She stands and drinks the water.

She shakes herself slightly, she goes back in.

and next?

ELECTRA next is my brother

AUDREY the same three always in the same order?

ELECTRA when I see him then I know it's about to start
that hell is coming
I think he and I should have shared them but somehow they
just come for me

AUDREY they always come after you have seen him?

ELECTRA yes

AUDREY where is your brother?

ELECTRA on a beach sometimes
  sometimes in a garden
  my brother can be anywhere

AUDREY the last time then?

ELECTRA he was here on a swing
  like there was a swing in this room
  sometimes he takes me in his arms sometimes he

AUDREY I can't see your brother can you describe him?

ELECTRA like me
  only taller
  same skin
  skinnier
  younger now
  pretty useless

  *A little boy, OWEN, comes in. He is about eight. He has
  a bouncy ball with him.*

AUDREY now wait a minute

ELECTRA something wrong?

AUDREY you don't belong in this

OWEN Audrey

ELECTRA what's happening?

AUDREY nothing keep talking, your brother

ELECTRA my brother is the only one that talks to me like he
  knows me

  A MAN's voice starts.

MAN you didn't even see him Audrey, he was playing with his ball

ELECTRA who's that?

AUDREY there seems to be something going on for me today

some crossed wires in my concentration

I am sorry I think I'm getting a migraine

MAN useless girl

he ran out behind me

AUDREY *looks.*

An older man, IAN, *who is drunk is leering at her.*

IAN you want me to prove to you, you are fucking nothing

and if you tell your aunt again

AUDREY can you pass some water Electra please?

ELECTRA *tries to pass her some water.*

AUDREY *looks around.*

and then the noises start...

ELECTRA only if you hear them too

AUDREY you tricked me

ELECTRA how could I?

AUDREY I am your doctor Electra, not the other way around

ELECTRA you said you'd never heard them

AUDREY I dealt with it

I had years of therapy

I was fifteen, I was a mess, yes but

ELECTRA they never stop

AUDREY they did for me

they did stop

The sniffing is getting louder, the howling wind.

shit

will you ring a bell Electra, will you get a nurse?

fucking hell.

The noises are all around her.

AUDREY *shouts at* **ELECTRA.**

what are you doing?

why aren't you getting a nurse?

ELECTRA you put me in restraints

AUDREY shout then

wait

where have you gone?

Electra?

Electra?

Don't leave me in this

Electra?

AUDREY *is on her own.*

She is frightened now. She looks all around her.

Her dad is in front of her.

IAN I didn't do it

you tell anyone I did it, and I will fucking knock you to the sky

AUDREY Dad

IAN I didn't do it

AUDREY there must be a way to make this stop

IAN he ran out behind the car

I wasn't drinking, I hadn't drunk anything.

you were in the front seat and were playing with the
handbrake
you're a little girl
nothing will happen to you if you say you were playing with
the handbrake

AUDREY I can't lie

IAN you haven't got a mother, what do you want to happen to you
you know what they do to children in care?
they eat them, they boil up their bones and serve them up
can you hear me Audrey?

Her brother comes in.

He plays with the ball.

OWEN another fifteen bounces and I break my record

IAN I was not in the car

OWEN he was drunk, again

IAN fathers need help Audrey sometimes

AUDREY I am not seven any more, please

OWEN he was drinking at breakfast

IAN I'm getting myself sorted, don't turn your back on me
Audrey

AUDREY stop it
this is a hallucination

IAN I've been going to my group

OWEN he is on the stairs

AUDREY I am a doctor, I am in a clinic

OWEN passed out

AUDREY some sort of projection, they are both dead

OWEN you are fourteen now, not a girl

AUDREY leave me alone

    please Owen

    someone ring the bell

OWEN he's on the stairs, passed out

IAN I need some help

    Audrey help an old man

AUDREY Electra can you reach the bell?

OWEN walk over him Audrey

IAN I'm vomiting

    I might choke

OWEN walk past him

IAN if you do that I'll die

OWEN you and me we can get through anything

AUDREY Electra is that you, has a nurse come in?

OWEN how many times are you going to clear up his vomit?

AUDREY Electra?

    ELECTRA *manages to speak to her through the hallucination.*

ELECTRA they never stop

AUDREY Electra, ring the bell

ELECTRA rope

    that is what we need

    rope is the only way out

AUDREY I can't do that

ELECTRA it's for us both

    AUDREY *stops.*

AUDREY get away from me

get away from me

this is not the way out

She pushes them away, the noises come back.

The sniffing, the barking, the laughing.

It feels so loud it's like your head might split.

AUDREY *is swirling around, this side and that.*

YOU HAD STOPPED,

YOU ...

The noises all around her become defeaning, like hell itself has come to call.

She screams.

AUDREY *screams and screams.*

Scene Eleven

MICHAEL *and* MEGAN *are talking over* AUDREY, *who is now in bed.*

MEGAN you should have made a report if you thought she was in danger

MICHAEL what signs were there?

MEGAN you knew her as a patient

MICHAEL years ago

MEGAN but didn't declare it?

MICHAEL do people not get a chance to start again?

she got through it

MEGAN her brother died in a road accident that she caused

MICHAEL no

MEGAN there's a report

we all know about it now

she was playing with the handbrake

if that isn't something dark in the cupboard of skeletons I

don't know what is

MICHAEL she wasn't in the car I believe

MEGAN and then later her father died on his own vomit

MICHAEL yes I am aware of the details

MEGAN if she was alone with him when he died

it's enough to make anyone permanently wobbly,

question mark over whether she was involved

you should have come clean

she changed her name but so what?

MICHAEL I thought she had come through it

MEGAN it's not my place but I would have thought you never
come through something like this

MICHAEL can't we keep it private, for a week or two?

MEGAN from the other staff?

MICHAEL this is Audrey
our brilliant star
this isn't just some patient

MEGAN we'll have to move her

MICHAEL no, we keep her here

MEGAN what about her new job?

MICHAEL I can't tell Ohio

MEGAN she isn't the person they thought they were getting

MICHAEL she might get back to there

MEGAN she can't practise again Michael, open your eyes
I blame myself

MICHAEL enough

MEGAN well you raised an awareness and we all knew about it

MICHAEL these things can't be predicted
something triggered old psychosis

MEGAN it happens
do you want to phone Ohio or should I?

MICHAEL can't we just leave it a week?
do you have to look so fucking gleeful?
this is someone's whole life going up the shitter Megan
I know there are things in your life that you are pretty
bloody sad about, but must everyone suffer because of your
pain?

MEGAN that's enough Michael

that is quite enough.

I'll ring Ohio straightaway.

She walks out.

MICHAEL *is left with* **AUDREY,** *and his sadness.*

He strokes her head.

Scene Twelve

AUDREY *is standing alone beside a window.*

ELECTRA *is standing beside hers.*

They aren't in the same space and yet somehow they are.

AUDREY why did you never manage?

ELECTRA I couldn't

AUDREY fear?

ELECTRA they wouldn't let me
    I tried
    I tried every which way
    I don't eat, I don't sleep
    I take the maximum strength everything
    I have lived so long my body should be long over
    and yet I look like a girl

AUDREY how long?

ELECTRA an eternity
    my race died out long ago
    everyone forgot me
    my family and what they did is just a story now

AUDREY is that what is in store for me?

ELECTRA I don't know

AUDREY I was free
    I hadn't thought about them for years
    I was living my life

ELECTRA they never go

AUDREY they did for me

ELECTRA they would have come back

in the end.

ELECTRA *looks up to the top of the window.*

there is a piece of rope inside the window frame.

AUDREY *looks up.*

inside it holds the sash up

AUDREY I see it

ELECTRA can you reach it?

AUDREY I think so

ELECTRA go on then

AUDREY but you said it didn't work

ELECTRA if we do it together

we are connected, somehow you and I

AUDREY Michael says everyone has a shadow

ELECTRA if we jump together

AUDREY and leave this?

ELECTRA it's not so much

torment and misery?

they won't let go, however hard we run

AUDREY is it a curse?

ELECTRA yes

we're cursed

Both of them at the same time reach up and reach for the piece of rope inside their window sash.

if you can loop it over

AUDREY are we dreaming?

ELECTRA I don't know

AUDREY they will have sedated me

will have put me in a ward on my own

Megan will have loved that

I'll probably be at the end of the corridor, the one near the nurses

ELECTRA take the sash Audrey

AUDREY we need a knife to cut it

there won't be a knife in this ward

ELECTRA no you can just tie a knot

put it over our heads

AUDREY we'll need a chair

ELECTRA we've got chairs

we've got everything we need

They both stand up on to the chairs.

They then put the sash around their necks.

They both stand there ready.

AUDREY are you ok Electra?

ELECTRA yes

are you?

AUDREY yes

They jump.

A bell starts to ring.

There are bells all around.

They seem to come from everywhere and are really loud.

Then they stop.

ELECTRA we did it

AUDREY free

ELECTRA wait

AUDREY what's that?

ELECTRA Doctor?

AUDREY where are we?

ELECTRA is that you?

AUDREY yes I'm here but there are others

ELECTRA there was going to be nothing

AUDREY I can't see you

ELECTRA I can hear you though

AUDREY I'm here

They are in a new place.

Chairs are being set up.

ELECTRA *looks around.*

maybe we are just dying maybe this is just the last bit of
brain activity

ELECTRA will it end?

AUDREY I imagine, yes soon

CLYTEMNESTRA *is front of her.*

CLYTEMNESTRA it never ends

ELECTRA you –

AUDREY oh god

CLYTEMNESTRA hell Electra is without end, that is the purpose
you don't get to jump free

ELECTRA my brother did

CLYTEMNESTRA he didn't put the knife in my belly

ELECTRA it isn't fair

CLYTEMNESTRA oh you want to argue with hell now?

AUDREY it's just the dying embers of your brain, don't panic

CLYTEMNESTRA not true

AUDREY a final hallucination

ELECTRA please Mum let me go

CLYTEMNESTRA it's not me, I told you

AUDREY hang on Electra, this will pass

CLYTEMNESTRA all that I can do is watch, even if I wanted to
stop it

People start to walk on to stage.

ELECTRA who are they?

AUDREY it's all in your mind

CHORUS you will have to clear a space

AUDREY me?

ELECTRA but I know you
you've been watching us all the way through

CHORUS exactly and this is our purpose

ELECTRA what purpose?

CHORUS your trial
we're the jury

CLYTEMNESTRA she doesn't get a trial, she has been condemned
already

CHORUS she appealed

CLYTEMNESTRA when did she appeal?

CHORUS she appealed to god

CLYTEMNESTRA which god, when I got here I found there were
none

CHORUS that is true, but nature heard her cry

you have to stand back madam

ELECTRA don't leave me Doctor

AUDREY I won't

CHORUS but your trial is later

AUDREY I get a trial too?

CHORUS not today some time from now

CLYTEMNESTRA there must be someone who has got this wrong

what do you mean by nature?

CHORUS older than the gods, and what will take over when
we are all gone

ELECTRA so my case will be heard?

CLYTEMNESTRA no need to celebrate

CHORUS it has been heard

that is why we watched

CLYTEMNESTRA the ill-fitting, the insane?

CHORUS who better?

the left behind

the malformed,

who else could nature trust?

One of the **CHORUS** *puts a box down.*

CLYTEMNESTRA you were deceitful then

CHORUS not at all

CLYTEMNESTRA said you were my friends

ELECTRA and mine also

CHORUS we were watchers yes

    objective, silent

CLYTEMNESTRA you should have said

CHORUS the votes have been counted

    it's time to listen

CLYTEMNESTRA I won't accept it whatever the outcome

CHORUS you have no choice

CLYTEMNESTRA not from you

CHORUS there is nothing bigger than nature

    the natural order of things

    of death and rebirth

    of love and hatred

    you have to accept the vote

    on one side Electra is a window

    you cannot see it

    but it is a window that will never close

    if the vote is counted and you are guilty, then there is

    nothing between you and torment for ever

    you'll be ripped around and torn to shreds by night, and

    restored by day only to have the same skin ripped off again

    when darkness comes.

    if the vote goes against you there will be no mercy then

ELECTRA is this still a hallucination Doctor?

AUDREY I don't know any more

ELECTRA and what's on the other side? you said there were

    two sides

CHORUS is sleep, gentle sleep

    at first

    the healing rest that you crave

ELECTRA and then?

CHORUS and then, it's up to you
    this modern world may not be to your liking but
    through that door is peace
    an end to torment

    ELECTRA *looks over.*

ELECTRA I can see it

CHORUS look away now.
    even a glimpse will tantalise

    Beat.

    will you both accept the count when it is made?
    there is no certainty of which way this will go

CLYTEMNESTRA how many watched?

CHORUS you saw us
    three in first instance, but another three
    and another three until we were many
    nature called us, come and watch

ELECTRA tell us the results then

CLYTEMNESTRA do I get a say, to put my case?

CHORUS you have had it
    everything has been said and said again

CLYTEMNESTRA so we just wait?

CHORUS while we count yes

    There's a noise.

    The sniffing and howling.

    keep them back, the verdict isn't out

CLYTEMNESTRA they are hungry, they want to play

ELECTRA you only say that to frighten me

CLYTEMNESTRA why would I frighten you? this is hell's doing
not mine

ELECTRA it suits you though, this destruction

CLYTEMNESTRA hush now, enough has been said

Some whispering among the CHORUS.

ELECTRA is there a problem?

More murmuring in the jury.

CLYTEMNESTRA you said it would be quick

CHORUS give us a second

ELECTRA well how long?

The CHORUS *talk among themselves.*

CHORUS can we go back?
    I can't see it all again
    and where would we start
    this sorry story is without a beginning
    we can't do it all over
    not again

CLYTEMNESTRA what's going on?

CHORUS count again

ELECTRA give us the news

CHORUS you'll have to wait a little longer

CLYTEMNESTRA but the hounds
    the window is already bulging

    They count again.

ELECTRA tell us what is happening?

CHORUS how can it be, we were an odd number?

it doesn't make sense

it comes out as many for one side as another

CLYTEMNESTRA count again

CHORUS we have counted

Electra killed her mother yes, but for reasons we can
understand

the child had no chance

there are others of us that feel she should be punished

CLYTEMNESTRA quite right

CHORUS and then again, others –

she was never loved like she should have been

we cannot agree, that is the long of it

we have debated for hours

if she had been allowed a proper childhood

plenty are denied a childhood but to take to murder

don't start arguing

who said I am arguing?

CLYTEMNESTRA so there is no conclusion at all?

CHORUS none it seems

or none that can be found here

ELECTRA what about the doctor, can she give a vote?

CHORUS she isn't here, Electra

she isn't part of this story

Beat.

ELECTRA *looks around.* **AUDREY** *has gone.*

ELECTRA Doctor?

CHORUS she's gone,

    this story has no end then

    there is no moral

    no conclusion

    did we fail?

    this restless house will stay stirring and vengeful

    there must be someone else who can pass a vote

    no one, who else could there be?

    tell the audience, we have come to the end but there is no

    conclusion

    that's rubbish

    apologies

    get your money back on the way out

    the story couldn't be finished

    we couldn't decide

    was Electra guilty or not? who knows!

    can't we count again?

    house lights up

    perhaps a song, and they won't notice

    can someone pick up a guitar

CLYTEMNESTRA what?

    this can't be it?

ELECTRA and what happens to me?

CHORUS I don't know, that's the whole point

    we can't finish

    the last scene will remain undone

CLYTEMNESTRA and me?

CHORUS I guess you go back to the beginning

    do it all again

or stay here perhaps stuck in this moment

A little girl comes on to stage in a yellow dress.

IPHIGENIA excuse me

CHORUS just a second

Beat.

IPHIGENIA excuse me

can I get past?

CHORUS where are you going?

IPHIGENIA to go and play

CHORUS what is she doing here?

this is a court

we can't have children playing

CLYTEMNESTRA can you stop this?

CHORUS is she part of the jury?

who is this girl?

you don't recognize her?

ELECTRA she's Iphigenia

CHORUS she also watched

CLYTEMNESTRA my baby?

CHORUS the first vengeful spirit

don't you remember?

CLYTEMNESTRA she should have the final vote

CHORUS it makes sense she should have the final vote, her death

started this story

CLYTEMNESTRA nature sent her to finish it

and nature would be on the side of mother and child

too bad Electra

IPHIGENIA can I play here?

Beat.

IPHIGENIA *sits down on the floor and opens the case.*

CLYTEMNESTRA stand up Iphigenia

ELECTRA this isn't fair

CHORUS she brought burdock for brutality
bilberry for bludgery
I remember now

CLYTEMNESTRA she sat on my back

ELECTRA exactly she was your creature, that isn't fair

CLYTEMNESTRA stand up

ELECTRA Sister is that you?

CLYTEMNESTRA remember your mother's pain at your passing

ELECTRA remember we share a blood

CHORUS remember to be fair Iphigenia

She stops, she looks around all of them.

She goes back to her case.

CLYTEMNESTRA you have to stand up

CHORUS you have to say something

CLYTEMNESTRA nature has given you the final vote, we've all
agreed

CHORUS this case matters most of all
if Electra is innocent, then perhaps all children will start to
murder their parents without fear of retribution
but if Electra is guilty

Beat.

CLYTEMNESTRA why won't she stand up?

CHORUS is she going to sit and play for ever

　　you were the first vengeance

IPHIGENIA I'll have no part in this

　　Beat.

CLYTEMNESTRA you climbed on my back

IPHIGENIA but I didn't

CLYTEMNESTRA what?

CHORUS we saw you

IPHIGENIA I didn't climb anywhere

CLYTEMNESTRA now wait

　　I have the marks where you clawed yourself in

IPHIGENIA I did nothing

　　if you thought I did

　　it was because you wanted to think that

　　I am a little girl

　　Mum

　　Dad

　　Is my father here too?

　　I was a little girl

　　I wanted to play with my dolls

　　I wanted to run on the sand

　　I was never a spirit of anything

CHORUS but in your suitcase –

IPHIGENIA there is nothing much in my suitcase

　　I was murdered yes but I never came back

ELECTRA you spoke to me as well

you whispered words into my ears
hibiscus, hawthorn

IPHIGENIA no
I did nothing
the living drive the living, not the dead
spirits and gods and demons, we've gone
no lasting impression, no power to change
can I play now?

CHORUS you won't vote?
she's said what she has said
must she say more?

IPHIGENIA my vote is for an end.
it's to stop
I was just a little girl
everything else was you.

MICHAEL *comes on, as if in a clinic.*

MICHAEL what is in your case little girl?

IPHIGENIA you know my story?

MICHAEL yes I have your notes

IPHIGENIA in my case
nothing really
a little poultice that my mummy made me, that helps me
sleep
and a little picture of my dad
and my sister is just a baby but she is here too
and my brother

CHORUS no hibiscus no hawthorn?

IPHIGENIA I have a toothbrush and a hair band

CHORUS no bilberry no burdock?

MICHAEL you keep them in your case?

IPHIGENIA yes I keep them all here

CHORUS no dandelion, no compfrey?

IPHIGENIA just my dolls and my toys

ELECTRA I remember now I had a case just like that
I can't remember what was in it

CHORUS poison and venom?

ELECTRA not at the start, before it got emptied

AGAMEMNON I had a case too, when I was a boy

AGAMEMNON *has appeared on stage.*

CHORUS we thought you were always a warrior

AGAMEMNON no there was a time before
it was more of a box than a case but, in it
if only I could remember what I did with it, I used to go
everywhere with it in my arms

CLYTEMNESTRA mine was a bag

AGAMEMNON I remember that

CLYTEMNESTRA you do?
a little pretty bag

ORESTES *comes on stage.*

ORESTES there was never enough in my case to be brief
it was always hollow

IPHIGENIA there are things in mine
would you like something?

Beat.

IPHIGENIA *gets things and offers it.*

I've got lots of things. A doll or a ball or
a game we could play together?

ORESTES I can take something from you?

IPHIGENIA why not, you're my brother. Do you want to play
a game?

I've got things for all of you.

AGAMEMNON *looks at* **CLYTEMNESTRA.**

you all need things, don't you? For you Dad, a special shell
for love that has been lost.

AGAMEMNON *takes it.*

I stuck a nail through it but it didn't crack. For my sister
plastic flowers to heal a grieving heart

She gives some plastic flowers to **ELECTRA.**

and for Mum a tin teapot and a plate of jewels

She hands this to her mother.

CLYTEMNESTRA what sort of jewels?

IPHIGENIA jewels I found by the beach
for you to put in your hair

IPHIGENIA *holds up some seaweed.*

CLYTEMNESTRA *deliberates, she takes the seaweed.*

then Daddy will tell you that you look beautiful and you
will smile. I have a teapot and three cups, I only have water
for the teapot but you can pretend it is any drink you want.

She hands her mother a cup. **CLYTEMNESTRA** *takes it.*

and you Dad, will you drink too?

CLYTEMNESTRA Electra?

ELECTRA Mum?

CLYTEMNESTRA *almost falls.*

CLYTEMNESTRA it's hard, I can feel those furies at my back

There is a sort of outbreath behind her.

IPHIGENIA it's just a game

CLYTEMNESTRA Electra?

ELECTRA we never played any games.

AGAMEMNON forgive her, let go

CLYTEMNESTRA as I am forgiven?

AGAMEMNON *nods, then collapses too.*

AGAMEMNON I can't in fact, it's too hard

ORESTES but possible, Dad I am by your side

IPHIGENIA you have to pretend it's tea
  you can stir the sugar in if you like and pretend it is
  peppermint and then on this plate is whatever you can
  imagine

CLYTEMNESTRA and then what?

ORESTES we just become ghosts, Electra is already dust

ELECTRA I'm dead?

ORESTES the rope held firm

CLYTEMNESTRA and them, the things out there?

IPHIGENIA I'll invite them in, give them tea. There is plenty
  for us all.

ELECTRA now wait a minute

IPHIGENIA they are only scary if you run from them. If you ask
  them in they sit down like friends. There is nothing to fear.

MICHAEL it's nearly the end of the clinic

I think we have got somewhere

are you happy to close your case little girl?

She nods.

I'll see you again then

A wind starts up.

He looks up at the skies.

next time.

MICHAEL *gets up to go, he leaves the ghosts drinking pretend cups of tea.*

Scene Thirteen

AUDREY *is in front of a window.*

She opens it wide.

AUDREY fly away.

JORDAN *comes beside her.*

JORDAN are you ok?

She nods.

AUDREY I wasn't

JORDAN you wouldn't go anywhere would you?

AUDREY of course not

maybe I came close but

JORDAN they said a patient died and if the nurse hadn't been there, you would have too

AUDREY I know

Beat.

I'm glad she was there

that she found me in time

I watched my father choke to death, and I didn't help him.

I'll always have to live with that.

but I can live.

I can live with it.

and look the window is open

Beat. She leans out.

She looks right out.

ABOUT THE AUTHOR

Zinnie Harris is a multi-award-winning playwright, screenwriter and theatre director. In 2017 she had three productions open simultaneously as part of the Edinburgh International Festival: *Meet Me At Dawn* premiered at the Traverse Theatre, while her new adaptation of Ionesco's *Rhinoceros* and a revival of her trilogy *This Restless House* both opened at the Royal Lyceum Theatre. *Meet Me At Dawn* and *Rhinoceros* received multiple nominations for the 2018 Critics, Awards for Theatre in Scotland and *This Restless House*, which first premiered at the Citizens Theatre in Glasgow (2016), was winner of Best New Play at the same awards in 2016 and shortlisted for the Susan Smith Blackburn Prize 2016/7. Other plays include *How to Hold Your Breath* at the Royal Court Theatre (2015), which won the 2016 Berwin Lee Award; *The Wheel* for the National Theatre of Scotland (2011), which was a joint winner of the 2011 Amnesty International Freedom of Expression Award and won a Fringe First; *Midwinter* for the RSC (2004), which won her an Arts Foundation Fellowship Award for playwriting; and *Further Than The Furthest Thing* at the National Theatre/Tron Theatre (2000/1), which won the Peggy Ramsay Playwriting Award, the John Whiting Award, a Fringe First, a special commendation from the Susan Smith Blackburn Award, and got her shortlisted for the *Evening Standard*'s Most Promising Playwright Award.

Recent directing work for theatre includes *Gut* (Traverse/National Theatre of Scotland, 2018), *A Number* (Lyceum, 2017) for which she won Best Director at the 2017 Critics, Awards for Theatre in Scotland.

Zinnie has also written for television and radio, with two ninety-minute dramas for Channel 4 called *Born With Two Mothers* and *Richard Is My Boyfriend* and episodes for the BBC One drama series *Spooks*. She was lead writer on the series *Partners In Crime* for Endor/BBC One (broadcast in 2015), starring Jessica Raine and David Walliams and which was based on the Agatha Christie Tommy and Tuppence novels, and is currently developing a new series for the BBC.

Zinnie is currently under commission to the Royal Court, the Royal Shakespeare Company and the Royal National Theatre. She was associate director at the Traverse Theatre from 2015–2018, and is the professor of playwriting and screenwriting at the University of St Andrews.

Other plays by ZINNIE HARRIS
published and licensed by Concord Theatricals

This Restless House
Agamemnon's Return
Based on Aeschylus' *Oresteia*

FIND PERFECT PLAYS TO PERFORM AT
www.concordtheatricals.co.uk